PERFORMANCE *Basics*

JOE WILLMORE

A Complete, How-to Guide to Help You:

▶ Understand Human Performance Improvement (HPI)

▶ Build Confidence to Adopt a Performance Approach

▶ Apply HPI to Your Practice or Organization

ASTD Press

ASTD Press is an internationally renowned source of insightful and practical information on workplace learning and performance topics, including training basics, evaluation and return-on-investment (ROI), instructional systems development (ISD), e-learning, leadership, and career development.

Ordering information: Books published by ASTD Press can be purchased by visiting our website at store.astd.org or by calling 800.628.2783 or 703.683.8100.

Library of Congress Control Number: 2004109346

ISBN-10: 1-56286-370-3
ISBN-13: 978-1-56286-370-8

Acquisitions and Development Editor: Mark Morrow
Copyeditor: Karen Eddleman
Interior Design and Production: Kathleen Schaner
Cover Design: Ana Ilieva
Cover Illustration: Phil and Jim Bliss

Printed by Victor Graphics, Inc., Baltimore, MD, www.victorgraphics.com

Table of Contents

About the
Training Basics Series

■ ■

ASTD's *Training Basics* series recognizes and, in some ways, celebrates the fast-paced, ever-changing reality of organizations today. Jobs, roles, and expectations change quickly. One day you might be a network administrator or a process line manager, and the next day you might be asked to train 50 employees in basic computer skills or to instruct line workers in quality processes.

Where do you turn for help? The ASTD *Training Basics* series is designed to be your one-stop solution. The series takes a minimalist approach to your learning curve dilemma and presents only the information you need to be successful. Each book in the series guides you through key aspects of training: giving presentations, making the transition to the role of trainer, designing and delivering training, and evaluating training. The books in the series also include some advanced skills such as performance and basic business proficiencies.

The ASTD *Training Basics* series is the perfect tool for training and performance professionals looking for easy-to-understand materials that will prepare non-trainers to take on a training role. In addition, this series is the perfect reference tool for any trainer's bookshelf and a quick way to hone your existing skills. The titles currently planned for the series include:

- ▶ *Presentation Basics* (2003)
- ▶ *Trainer Basics* (2003)
- ▶ *Training Design Basics* (2003)
- ▶ *Facilitation Basics* (2004)
- ▶ *Communication Basics* (2004)
- ▶ *Performance Basics* (2004)
- ▶ *Evaluation Basics* (2005)
- ▶ *Needs Assessment Basics* (2005)
- ▶ *ROI Basics* (2005).

Preface

■ ■

Early in my training career, I was hired by a client to provide training on motivation to a group of employees. As I prepared for the course, I discovered the reason they were being given the motivational training was that they had been given 90 days to improve their performance or they would be dismissed. As part of this arrangement, all employees given the 90-day warning received training on motivation and either technical or skills training focused in areas where their performance was below par. Historically, however, people who had been given their 90-day notice somehow never managed to get off the termination list.

Desperate to do a good job with this client, I visited the worksite to observe the workers in question in the hope I could find ways to adapt the training well enough to at least earn good evaluations because it certainly didn't look as if my training was going to help people keep their jobs or improve their performance.

What I discovered by observing their work was that none of the employees in question could see their computer screens very well. The overhead lighting was inadequate. To compensate they had to rely on outside lighting, which produced excessive glare. These were the days of early word processors when screens were monochrome and difficult to read, even under the best of conditions. This environment caused a high percentage of document errors to go unnoticed by the staff.

The solution in this case wasn't training. By improving the quality of the indoor lighting and adding glare screens, performance improved dramatically. Errors that had previously gone undetected by the employees suddenly became noticeable when they could read their screens. Interestingly enough, the only way I could get paid for my contribution was to go ahead and conduct the training on motivation. This was my first professional insight involving performance improvement: Training is not the answer to many problems faced by organizations.

How Can This Book Help?

You've probably heard from managers or peers (or through reading ASTD research reports on trends in the industry) that the movement to performance is strong and pervasive. Simply put, all kinds of organizations worldwide are focusing on results. Trainers are being held accountable by managers for organizational results. They must be able to show their value on the organization's bottom line. The movement to performance is not going away any time soon. So, if you're trying to find out more information about what this performance movement is all about, how it applies to you, and how you can start applying performance improvement to your work, then this book is for you.

This book is specifically written for people who have little or no formal background in performance consulting, are just getting started in it, or need to find out more information about what it involves. There is little emphasis on theory, models, or historical background. The focus is on the practical application of performance improvement. Additionally, this book is designed to be consistent in approach, terminology, and content with ASTD's Human Performance Improvement (HPI) certificate training seminars.

Acknowledgments

This book could not have been written without the support, advice, and wisdom of many people. There are a host of performance consultants who have entertained my foolish questions and offbeat thoughts over the years while patiently explaining the errors of my ways. I have to thank Dana Robinson, Paul Elliott, Tom LaBonte, Jim Fuller, Ethan Sanders, Jeff Parks, Mary Broad, George Piskurich, Geary Rummler, Phil Anderson, Don Ford, Dennis Mankin, and Rebecca Birch for their wisdom and insights. Through conversations and email exchanges they've broadened my understanding of what it means to be a performance consultant, and their contributions are reflected in the advice contained in this book. They constitute a very diverse group of performance consultants. Last of all, I wish to thank my wife, Cathy, for her ability to tolerate both me and the writing process.

Joe Willmore
October 2004

1

The Big Picture:
Why Focus on
Performance Improvement?

What's Inside This Chapter

Here you'll see how to:

▶ Identify implications of the performance improvement
  movement for trainers and others in the human resource
  development (HRD) field
▶ Get started in performance consulting
▶ Understand the emphasis placed on performance
▶ Navigate this book and its structure to find specific
  information
▶ Use the icons as a guide to special material in this book.

How Performance Basics Can Help You

You've probably heard from a range of sources that the training profession is focusing
more on performance. Perhaps senior management has started to put pressure on your
training department to "quantify the impact" of the training you do or to demonstrate
the "return on the company's investment." Maybe you feel that the training you provide is valuable but you'd like to have even more impact on the organization. Or, it's

possible you've been told by senior management that you're going to start doing performance consulting. In any case, this book will help you.

Many misconceptions swirl around the area of performance improvement. When you hear that the human development field is moving to more of a performance focus, it is only natural to question the permanence of this focus shift. Perhaps you or your organization has already decided that you're going to be more of a performance consultant. Whether or not you intend to do performance consulting, this is an area that is crucial for you to understand, and it's also one that isn't that difficult to get started in. Performance improvement has meant and will continue to mean sweeping changes for those in the training and development professions. Anyone who wants to be a professional trainer needs to understand what human performance improvement (HPI) is all about and the implications for the training profession.

Noted

Performance consultants aren't the only ones who can benefit by studying HPI. Even if you know you won't be in a performance consulting role, being knowledgeable about this field can help you do your current job better.

Maybe you've already noticed the trend toward performance in your profession. ASTD—the world's largest society of workplace learning and performance professionals—has certainly concluded that a shift to performance is a key trend in today's workplace. Research findings by other organizations match ASTD's conclusions. This increasing emphasis on performance only mirrors forces that are going on elsewhere in the world.

Starting in the mid-1980s, there has been a shift in the United States within the field of education to an increased emphasis on performance (and thus the use of testing to evaluate and establish accountability). Performance-based budgeting and accountability are increasing trends within government. Almost all professional fields are placing a greater emphasis and accountability on performance. Even civil engineering is seeing greater emphasis on performance-based design.

Furthermore, this push for performance accountability is not a recent phenomenon. The human performance improvement field has been around professionally as a recognized area of study for decades, and the basic roots of this field go back even further (Sanders and Ruggles, 2000). In short, increasing attention on performance is not a fad; it won't go away, and it will become more pervasive. Organizations and management are asking for human development professionals to be more accountable for performance results, and the training profession is moving more toward a performance focus. So, trainers who aren't performance savvy will find themselves out of step with their profession, their clients, their management, and their organization.

Why is the emphasis on performance and results increasing? The simple answer is that most human performance issues can't be solved by training. Training addresses performance gaps caused by a lack of skill or knowledge, but training cannot improve motivation; change job designs, workflow, organizational structure; or solve a host of other factors.

Noted

ASTD found in its two most recent trends reports that an increased emphasis on performance was one of the top 10 trends relevant to training and development professionals.

Research tells us that more than 80 percent of the time performance problems aren't caused by a lack of skills or knowledge within the performer. Studies by Edward Deming, Paul Elliott, Joe Harless, and others have repeatedly shown that while there are a variety of causes for poor results by performers, training doesn't solve the majority of them. When asked to self-assess individual performance gaps, very few performers identify a lack of skills or knowledge as the primary barrier to improving their performance (Dean, Dean & Rebalsky, 1996).

In short, a wide variety of research findings show that training isn't the solution to most performance gaps because the vast majority of poor performance is not due to poor skills or lack of knowledge; it's a result of other causes such as process problems, motivation, incentive issues, resources, unclear standards, or confusing feedback. Training addresses a lack of knowledge or poor skills but not the other areas, and that means training won't solve the vast majority of human performance problems at work.

Noted

Joe Harless, one of the leaders and practitioners of performance improvement, found that out of 200 analyses conducted across a wide range of organizations to determine the cause and the solution for performance gaps, the most frequent cause was the lack of adequate feedback. The most infrequent cause of poor performance was lack of skills or knowledge by the performers involved. Training won't solve most performance issues at work.

This is critical concept for you to master as a trainer, organization development (OD) practitioner, or any other professional in the human development field. Poor performance can be due to any number of factors, but many organizations continue to throw training at all or most performance issues. This inappropriate reliance upon training interventions is a losing proposition for everyone concerned: It wastes vital organizational resources, builds a bad reputation for the training department (because the problems you're told to solve don't go away), and increases cynicism within the workforce.

Basic Rule 1

Although organizations tend to rely upon training as a one-size-fits-every-problem answer, it is not always the solution to a performance gap. Nevertheless, trainers may be held accountable for the results of inappropriate training interventions.

As a trainer, you won't be able to help the organization with the vast majority of performance gaps, thus minimizing your value; and the organization is likely to ask you to solve many performance issues you have no hope of solving for the aforementioned reasons. Though you know your impact may be minimal within the organization, you will still be held accountable for the results. This is clearly a no-win situation: Trainers are asked to solve problems with training that are not covered in the scope of training's capabilities. Faced with such a situation, you can say "no" to the majority of client requests. The other option is to improve your ability to understand performance gaps and how to solve them when they don't involve training issues.

Becoming more performance focused in your work shouldn't happen just because management is pressuring training to move in that direction or

Think About This

Because of increasing emphasis on performance within organizations, more people in our profession have begun calling themselves "performance consultants" although they continue to operate as before. Performance consulting involves some fundamental changes in the way performance issues are approached with clients. It's not enough to just change your job title.

because of professional trends. Whether management has gotten on the performance train or not, there is a perfectly compelling case for you to become more performance focused in your work approach. Taking a performance focus to your work means being significantly more effective in whatever you do, and it also means that you spend more time and resources on issues that are mission critical to the organization (and thus have a much higher return), and you're also much more successful with the work you do take on. As a result, you'll be seen as invaluable to the organization. Besides, who does not want to feel that the work he or she does is not a waste of time? In short, being performance focused means making more of a difference in your work.

Noted

Some organizations have decided to get into the performance consulting field by announcing to their clients that this is what they do and then sending the staff identified as future performance consultants to some kind of training. Being an effective performance consultant means more than just acquiring some new skills and knowledge. If you continue to operate as before (with only a change in job title from trainer to performance consultant), then you won't significantly improve performance, and clients will continue to respond to you as a trainer. As a performance consultant, you'll change how you operate with clients in a fundamental way.

Who Can Benefit From This Book?

At this point, you may have already decided that it's critical to know much more about performance consulting. However, if you're still undecided on how this material applies to you, here's an explanation of how an instructional designer, trainer, facilitator, or OD practitioner benefits from knowledge of performance consulting. First, the performance consulting process is a tool for evaluating performance gaps and designing solutions. Even if you're limited in your role to doing only one kind of solution (such as being an instructional designer or delivering stand-up training on specific topics), an awareness of performance consulting will improve your ability to do those specific functions.

Additionally, knowledge of performance consulting will help you avoid taking on problems that you can't solve. It is a waste of the organization's resources (and your time) to attempt to solve problems that don't involve lack of knowledge or skills; in addition, your clients will eventually come to regard you as a poor trainer because you keep providing training but nothing changes. Even if you can't deviate from the set of solutions assigned to you (such as training or OD), knowledge of performance consulting can increase your success rate by giving you the insight to identify problems that you are capable of addressing. It's in your own self-interest to be able to target the performance gap and its causes so you can steer your client to a solution that will be more efficacious and will give you a successful outcome.

Noted

You'll read and hear the terms "internal" practitioner and "external" consultant. An internal is someone employed by an organization to serve the employees of that organization. An external is someone whose clients are outside of the organization. This book uses language and examples more consistent with internal performance consultants, but the content is equally appropriate for both roles.

There are a number of different people who will benefit from this book. If you are new to performance consulting, this book will be a good introduction. If you're a training manager or HR director who's responsible for overseeing the performance function as part of your portfolio, then this book will be useful. It can help you understand the performance consulting role, how it fits in with the other services your department provides, and some of the issues regarding working together effectively. After all, you can't just add HPI as another service to your department. If you're a trainer, instructional designer,

Think About This

Regardless of your organizational role, being knowledgeable about performance improvement can improve your ability to do your job. It will also allow you to use your resources (staff, time, budget) much more wisely.

facilitator, HR professional, OD practitioner, quality consultant, or line manager who may have to interact with performance consultants, this book is for you. This book will also be a useful introduction if you're planning on taking ASTD's HPI certificate workshops.

What This Book Can Do for You

After you're done reading this book, you should understand how performance consultants approach problems, how your individual function can fit within an HPI framework, and how performance consulting is different from how you currently approach problems. If you're going to be held accountable for results—for actually eliminating performance gaps—then this book can help you do that. This book also helps you deal with client requests and gives you a better sense of how to partner to get work done. You'll also learn how to be more strategic and less transactional in your work. But—to be very clear—this book is not just for people who will be doing performance consulting work. Even if your current role is narrow and limited in focus, an awareness of how to improve performance will allow you to do your work more effectively and help you avoid taking on problems that can't be solved by your area of focus.

Think About This

Some of the most successful performance consultants don't have a reference to performance in their job titles and their clients don't even consider them to be in the performance field. Performance consultants can be successful without having to sell clients on the approach. Oftentimes this makes sense because they don't have to deal with selling clients on a new model, label, or job title, and they never have to explain how it's different from what they used to do.

This book is intended to introduce you to the field of performance improvement. Because it takes a very practical approach, you'll find scant reference to theories, models, or history. However, there are many tools, resources, tips, and examples.

Icons to Guide You

This book has plenty to offer in the way of content that can help you every day. Some icons will alert you to key features of the book. Here are the ones you'll find throughout all of the Training Basics series:

What's Inside This Chapter?

Each chapter opens with a short summary that serves as a quick reference to the chapter contents. Use this section to identify the information in the chapter and, if you wish, skip ahead to the material that is most useful to you.

Think About This

These are helpful tips that you can put in your back pocket to pull out when needed in preparation for or during facilitation.

Basic Rules

These rules cut to the chase. They are unequivocal and important concepts for facilitators.

Noted

This icon flags sections with greater detail or an explanation about a concept or a principle. Sometimes it is also used for a short, productive tangent.

Getting It Done

The final section of each chapter supports your ability to take the content of that chapter and apply it to your situation. The focus of this section is mostly on job aids and tools for understanding the content. Sometimes this section contains a list of questions for you to ponder, sometimes it is a self-assessment tool, and sometimes it is a list of action steps you can take to improve your skills and help increase the chances for participant success.

By the time you're finished with this book, you'll have a very good understanding of what performance consulting is, how it's relevant to what you do, and how to proceed to build your skills and knowledge.

Getting It Done

This chapter provided you with a quick introduction and explained why performance consulting (regardless of your formal position in the organization) is relevant to you. There are plenty of reasons to become more knowledgeable about performance even if you won't be in a performance consulting role. Exercise 1-1 will help you determine your motivational factors for embarking on this tour of performance consulting and position you for the rest of this book.

Exercise 1-1. Getting set for tackling the rest of the book.

Here are some additional things you can do that will position you for the rest of this book:

1. Identify some examples of requests you received from clients for specific solutions (such as an order from management to provide listening skills training for the salesforce or a team-building session for a group of managers) in which the solution wasn't going to solve the problem. These are examples where a performance-focused approach would have avoided wasted resources by the organization.

2. Think of how your role may have changed in the past several years. What is expected from this position now as opposed to the past? In what ways do you expect your role to change in the future? By identifying how your role may be in transition, you can determine what aspects of performance consulting may be more relevant to your role or may be worth a greater focus on your part.

(continued on page 10)

Exercise 1-1. Getting set for tackling the rest of the book (continued).

3. What examples do you see within your organization or with your clients that show increased accountability for performance or pressure to demonstrate results? In what ways has your organization changed how the solutions you provide are evaluated: Is there more pressure to demonstrate return-on-investment (ROI) or show changes in business numbers because of your work? Is there more pressure on your training budget? These are forces within the organization that are compelling more of a performance focus.

4. In what way have your clients' expectations changed? What is different in terms of the results they want, how they want the work done, the pressure they face, or the process they want to use? As clients face more pressure to demonstrate results, that pressure is likely passed on to you (with more emphasis on quick results, justifying budget, or proving a clear value to the organization).

Answering the questions in the exercise helped you identify what aspects of performance consulting are especially relevant for you, the availability of performance consulting work that is applicable to your current clients, and possible ways to sell performance consulting to your clients or manager by connecting it to their immediate priorities.

The next chapter will provide you with an introduction of what performance consulting is and the key competencies and roles for effective performance consulting work. By the end of chapter 2, you'll have a good sense of what it means to be a performance consultant and how that work compares to what you currently do.

2

What Is Performance Consulting?

What's Inside This Chapter

Here you'll see how to:

▶ Identify common misconceptions about performance improvement
▶ Define performance consulting and discover what distinguishes it from other areas such as training, OD, facilitation, or quality improvement
▶ Discover what kinds of competencies and skills are valuable for performance consultants
▶ Distinguish performance consulting work from what you currently do
▶ Change how you do your work by applying a performance focus.

Defining Performance Consulting

Before defining performance consulting or performance focus, it's useful to discuss a few terms. The performance literature uses several different terms that have some relationship to performance improvement. Some examples are HPI, human performance technology (HPT), performance consulting, performance focus, human performance engineering, performance orientation, and performance approach. Although some people prefer one term over another, calling themselves performance consultants or performance technologists or HPI specialists, this book uses these terms interchangeably.

Noted

Dana and Jim Robinson (1996) first popularized the term performance consulting. *Prior to their book,* Performance Consulting: Moving Beyond Training, *it would have been more typical to refer to this profession as HPT or performance engineering.*

So if HPI, HPT, performance consulting, performance focus, performance orientation, and performance approach are basically synonyms, what do they mean? *HPI (or performance consulting) is a systematic and systemic approach to meeting organizational goals by identifying and closing human performance gaps.* Systematic means that consultants don't jump to conclusions or act prematurely. On the contrary, a performance approach requires a root cause analysis that not only identifies the performance gap, but what the real causes of the performance gap are. Think of times managers or clients have prematurely grasped a solution without any effort to identify the true cause of the problem. This situation is what a systematic approach is designed to counter.

Think About This

Whether people say they do HPI, HPT, or performance consulting is less important than using a term that has relevance to their clients.

A systematic approach also involves looking at a range of possible causes, withholding immediate judgment, and minimizing bias so that all of the relevant factors that may be contributing to the performance problem are considered. For instance, just because the employees could improve their skills or knowledge doesn't mean that is the primary cause of the performance issues and that training is the most effective way to address the gap. A systematic approach is a rigorous one that doesn't prematurely try to solve the problem and avoids bias in analyzing what is going on. This type of approach takes several factors into account (not just knowledge and skill improvement), and it doesn't assume that client requests are automatically the appropriate answer. In addition, a systematic approach also involves avoiding your own biases and being objective in how you evaluate performance data. You'll learn how to do all of this in later sections of this book.

Basic Rule 2

Performance consultants don't just focus on one possible cause for a performance problem or jump to conclusions. When analyzing performance gaps, it is their job to be rigorous and unbiased.

A systemic approach is one that looks at how the system contributes to the problem. For instance, when HPI consultants spot a performance gap, they will examine a range of possible root causes. Trainers focus on improving the knowledge and skills that would address these causes, because they are the only areas their training will target. But, if the primary reasons for the performance gaps are not knowledge or skill based, then training cannot correct the problem. For example, the source of the problem can be related to lack of or insufficient motivation, poor job design, or inaccuracy of system information, none of which are addressed by training. Thus, a systemic approach recognizes that to be successful it's important to look at the entire system to identify the causes of a performance problem and identify a solution.

A systemic approach also involves looking at how the organization affects successful implementation of the solution. It doesn't matter if training will solve the problem if the workers go back to the job to face resistance from managers when they try to apply the training. A systemic approach involves understanding the system—not only to identify the problem's causes but also to seek ways to achieve the desired changes. This part of the approach targets issues that might occur in management and tackles those issues. It isn't enough to provide the right solution, you must figure out how to make this solution accepted and implemented by the system.

The next element in the definition of HPI is meeting organizational goals. You may be under the impression that everyone does that, but that is not quite true. Most human resources activities in organizations are transactional, meaning that the

Basic Rule 3

Performance consultants are systemic and systematic in their work. They look at how the organizational system operates to understand why performance breaks down. They also recognize that to change performance problems they need to consider the entire system.

activities happen because someone else requests it. For instance, most training is transactional—the training department views its role as providing the training requested by one or more clients. Training provides classes and people sign up for them, or the client (such as a departmental manager) requests specific training content for specific staff within the department.

It's assumed that the training must be a good thing. After all, doesn't the client know what's best? If the clients get what they want, then isn't the training department doing a good job? That approach is not performance focused. Frequently, requests are made that are not based in reality. This includes times when the client has failed to consider what the real cause of the problem is or no consideration has been given as to whether or not the problem is even important enough to address.

Clients often request training for reasons that have very little to do with organizational priorities. These reasons could include any of the following: a desire to participate in the hottest new trend, an inability to describe what the real problem is, an eagerness to avoid responsibility for solving the problem by passing it on to someone else, an intention to reward employees by making training available, a need to show senior management some action on the problem, or as an indirect means of punishing staff by requiring them to all attend mandatory training.

Noted

Providing training—or any other service—for clients because they ask for it is a transactional approach. When trainers are transactional, they are not being performance focused or strategic. Performance consultants are not transactional.

Suppose a client requests a team-building intervention because the team is performing poorly. An interview of the team members shows that the team does indeed function badly. Does the team-building intervention meet organizational goals by improving the team? No, it doesn't. There is no indication

Basic Rule 4

Performance consultants focus on business goals. This is always the starting point for performance work; and without this business focus component, it is not performance consulting.

that team effectiveness (assuming the training or team building is successful) is the primary factor in whether the department meets its goals; therefore, there is no way to determine if the intervention will aid the meeting of organizational goals.

To meet organizational goals, the performance consultant must confirm what the goals are and determine what human performance is critical to meeting those goals. In so doing, the consultant is able to separate important performance issues from irrelevant or minor ones. While all organizations are full of performance issues that could be improved, most of those issues are not key drivers for important goals. Thus, HPI starts with organizational goals and identifies the performance that drives the goals.

Think About This

Performance consultants always find out what the key organizational goals are from their clients. Clients may start by talking about the solutions they want, but performance consultants always seek a way to bring the conversation to the goals the client needs to achieve or the targets for which the client is held accountable. For instance, consultants can indicate to the clients that more background is necessary or that context on the workers is important as one way of changing the conversation from a transactional focus.

To determine if performance consultants are meeting organizational goals, they need to evaluate their impact within the organization. A common way of categorizing different types of evaluation was developed by Donald Kirkpatrick (1975). Kirkpatrick's approach involves four levels of evaluation. Level 1 evaluation refers to reaction (or the postcourse evaluation sheets participants usually fill out). Level 2 refers to learning, with regard to the skills or knowledge that participants acquired in the course. Level 3 refers to behavior or application, meaning the degree to which participants apply what they learned from class to their work. Level 4 refers to impact or results (the degree to which organizational goals are met or business numbers change). Jack Phillips (1991) has now added what is sometimes referred to as level 5 or return-on-investment (ROI).

Most training departments have participants provide their reaction to the training (level 1 evaluation). If the services provided are transactional, then a level 1 measurement is usually sufficient. A good response on level 1 evaluation usually means participants are happy, and transactional trainers assume that happy participants mean a job well done. However, to determine if the organization got closer to meeting its goals, it's necessary to go beyond level 1 evaluation. Therefore, a performance focus usually involves level 4 evaluation or even an ROI analysis to quantify the bottom-line impact on the organization. Such an evaluation goes far beyond merely asking training participants if they liked the course materials or if the trainer demonstrated mastery in the subject.

The last part of the definition of HPI refers to the identification and closure of performance gaps. A performance gap is a discrepancy between current and desired accomplishments by workers. Such a gap could be with existing performance (workers aren't meeting expectations) or future performance (everyone's doing fine now but management is going to raise the bar and expects everyone to perform beyond current levels).

The process of identifying and closing performance gaps is not as easy as it sounds. Management may demand particular solutions, claiming, "My staff is too inefficient! They need time management training!" That demand isn't a performance gap—just a request for a particular solution (in this case, time management training). Performance consultants sometimes have to help management figure out what the actual performance gap is. Specifically, they'll need to identify what the results or accomplishments are that the performers are accountable for and how much of a discrepancy there is between the current performance and the expected levels. Oftentimes, this may get into issues about what is actually expected of workers and how it's measured.

Closing the performance gap means coming up with a solution to address the root causes of the gap, implementing the solution, and then evaluating how much success was had in eliminating the gap. Since a performance focus means taking on more issues than just knowledge or skills gaps, a lot of the intervention design and delivery will involve someone other than the performance consultant. Also, it probably isn't cost effective to implement every solution related to the problem because many performance gaps have 10 or 12 causes with numerous solutions, so to implement all of them isn't realistic. Remember: Because the focus is on meeting organizational goals, evaluation usually focuses on what kind of progress is made organizationally and, thus, determines grounds for evaluation.

Basic Rule 5

Performance consulting involves measurement to determine to what extent you've been able to close the performance gap and meet business objectives.

With increased emphasis on performance, professionals need to assess where they stand in terms of performance accountability. You have probably encountered others who insist that they have a performance focus in their work or that they're performance consultants. And yet what they do appears to be identical to what traditional trainers do. So, what's the difference? After talking about what performance consulting is, it will probably help to address what performance consulting isn't.

There is a tendency to assume that because performance is about results, if someone gets good results then he or she must have a performance focus or is practicing performance consulting. Or, to put it another way, if Linda is a trainer and her training improves performance then she must be a performance consultant—right? Absolutely not. Whether or not performance improves does not determine if someone has a performance focus to his or her work. Being good at what you do (whether it's training, OD, facilitation, quality assessment, or instructional design) does not make you a performance consultant.

Noted

Whether you succeed or fail with your work does not mean you're a performance consultant. Whether or not you do HPI is about the process you use to pick solutions for problems. As you'll probably discover, many people insist that they do performance improvement work although they actually have no idea what performance consulting means.

Consultants often do everything to the best of their ability but still come up short. It may be because the problems they were dealing with were insurmountable. Other possible reasons for the failure are that their organizations pulled away key resources at critical moments or that the organization lost interest in the problem. At times, consultants succeed because the problems were easy or they just got lucky. Success or failure with performance does not determine if someone is a performance consultant. How professionals go about approaching performance problems and the process used is what determines whether they are taking a performance consulting approach. Consequently, many people who insist that they do performance consulting are actually misinformed.

Basic Rule 6

The range of solutions or interventions you are capable of providing does not determine if you are a performance consultant. Performance consulting is not about being able to do things other than training.

Another misconception is the belief that your choice in the solutions you use to solve problems determines your status as a performance consultant. For instance, some professionals might insist they are performance consultants because they do more than training. That is not a determining factor. Whether or not someone is a performance consultant is not based on the range of solutions provided by the consultant. Focusing on actions consultants take or the solutions consultants provide clients is a transactional approach. Focusing on transactions leads to a mindset that the objective of work is to keep the customers happy, and the way to keep customers happy is to give them what they ask for. Instead, by focusing on performance results and following a performance consulting process, HR professionals can consistently generate good results. Again, performance consultants don't define themselves by what solutions they provide but by the process they use to determine what solutions will solve a particular performance problem.

The Four Key Roles of Performance Consultants

After examining what performance consulting is (and what it isn't), it's important to know the skills and competencies a good performance consultant needs to be

Think About This

There may be other groups that overlap somewhat with the performance function such as the OD, Six Sigma, or quality offices. One way to distinguish these groups from HPI is to determine if they identify themselves by the interventions they do or do not provide. For instance, if the OD center does not provide training, the OD consultants are defining who they are by the interventions they provide and not by the process that they use to achieve their solutions.

successful. Competencies refer to the key abilities required by a profession. Being a successful performance consultant involves some core competencies that go beyond those expected of a successful trainer, OD practitioner, or facilitator.

It's difficult to talk about what competencies all performance consultants need because the roles and functions of a performance consultant vary from organization to organization. The four key roles that performance consultants play can be labeled as analyst, intervention specialist, change manager, and evaluator (Rothwell, 1999).

Performance consultants fill one or more of the four key roles (Rothwell, 1999). Some performance consultants are responsible for all four roles, while others specialize in a combination of the four. The roles played by a performance consultant depend upon his or her organization, how the performance function is structured, and the kind of performance challenges he or she sees. In any case, each performance consultant role involves different competencies (although there is some overlap among competencies between roles). Thus, the role(s) a performance consultant is responsible for determines what competencies are necessary for work (table 2-1).

Analyst

The first role is that of the analyst (Rothwell, 1999). The analyst is a performance detective. This is the role responsible for the initial contact with the client and identifying what the performance gap is. Thus, the analyst does a lot of investigation and research to determine what the problem is. However, the analyst is not responsible for designing and delivering the solution. One competency that is important for analysts involves front-end analysis skills. Front-end analysis is the process of

Table 2-1. Key performance consulting roles.

Analyst	Determines business goals and performance gaps, and conducts root cause analysis leading to recommendations for action to improve performance.
Intervention Specialist	Manages or advises solution teams in the design, development, and delivery of specific solutions. The intervention specialist usually has expertise in the solution.
Change Manager	Coordinates implementation and rollout of solutions, especially complex or big efforts that may involve multiple initiatives. Also works to build buy-in and support.
Evaluator	Measures progress on several levels. Some data gathering may be used to improve the initiatives; other data collection focuses on assessment of organizational progress or value.

identifying the performance gap and comparing actual versus ideal performance. Another key competency for this role is questioning skills because this work involves gathering information from performers.

Analysts also need to be good at synthesis—the ability to integrate diverse data into a coherent whole. Analysts usually gather information from a variety of sources (such as interviews, focus groups, surveys, observation, and document review), and once all this information is pooled, then a more complete insight to the performance gap can be gained. Therefore, the ability to take these diverse perspectives and create a clear picture is critical.

Intervention Specialist

The second role of performance consulting is that of an intervention specialist (Rothwell, 1999). Intervention specialists may design and implement the solution,

Basic Rule 7

Analysts gather data to determine what is important to the organization, what performance gaps exist, how relevant those gaps are to critical business goals, and the causes of those performance gaps. This is typically referred to as front-end analysis.

Noted

Depending upon the performance consulting setup within an organization, the analyst role may also be responsible for the initial client contact of a project. This contact may be reactive (initiated by the client) or proactive (initiated by the consultant). Referred to as the contracting, engagement, partnering, or project alignment phase of the project (Block, 1981), this phase involves managing initial client contact, setting expectations for the project, and defining initial roles and responsibilities.

or they may supervise a contractor or expert who designs and delivers the solution. One other possibility is that the intervention specialist may coordinate a team of people who help create the solution (this may be especially true for distance learning courses that may involve a team of subject matter experts, information technology (IT) and programming staff, instructional designers, graphic designers, and multimedia staff). In any case, the intervention specialist is someone with particular expertise of the solution and some degree of project management skills.

Basic Rule 8

Intervention specialists either focus on the design and delivery of a specific kind of solution, or they manage a focused project to design and deliver a particular solution.

There are a number of competencies that are important to the role of intervention specialist. The intervention specialist needs to be able to take the information generated by the analyst and make enough sense from it to be able to design (or guide the design) of possible solutions. It is key that the intervention specialist be able to interpret information. The intervention specialist may also have to coordinate multiple solution projects on the same problem; and, as a result, another key competency for this role is the ability to assess relationships among interventions.

Noted

One significant change for many trainers or OD consultants who get into performance consulting is that they end up designing and delivering fewer solutions. To the extent they are involved in creating and delivering the solution, performance consultants often guide someone else to design and deliver the solutions. This happens because, as a performance consultant, their time will be so valuable it makes sense to have others handle actual delivery of many solutions.

Change Manager

The third role of the performance consultant is that of change manager (Rothwell, 1999). Managing change is a part of any performance improvement project—even very small ones of limited scope and focus. However, this role is more likely to serve as a distinct or specialized role for performance consultants on very large and diverse projects. For instance, if the performance gap involved several thousand performers with multiple interventions (training, job aids, changes in appraisal processes, revising organizational policies, and reengineering feedback processes), then the value of a dedicated change manager becomes much more obvious.

Basic Rule 9

The change manager may coordinate numerous solutions. In addition, he or she is responsible for working with implementation and buy-in strategies. This may include other changes in the client organization that are at odds with the proposed solutions.

With any given solution, almost always some elements of the organization create problems for that intervention. For instance, suppose that you are called to address a performance gap caused by work bottlenecks. The work bottlenecks develop because key staff members are called away for meetings, thus resulting in a work pileup. Your solution is to organize the work in teams so that team members can cover for people who are away. The problem is that this solution by itself will probably fail without a strong focus on change management. For example, if the organization still has a performance appraisal system that evaluates everyone individually as opposed to evaluating them as a team, it will work against the team setup by penalizing real team players who sacrifice individual glory for the good of the team. A good change manager would identify other elements of the system that need to be changed so that they support the proposed solution.

A good change manager also needs to deal with resistance to change. It may be necessary to set up and conduct meetings with employees to provide information and gain feedback about the proposed change. A combination of staff members and customers may choose to fight the change, and the change manager must be ready to deal with this resistance. Development of a communication plan is always an important part of an intervention or series of solutions, and a change manager will often coordinate the development and implementation of such a plan. Most changes encounter unexpected obstacles consisting of unanticipated issues, breakdowns in the intervention, or unplanned resistance. The change manager will usually play a big role in dealing with these intervention potholes.

Given the previous description, you can probably guess at some of the key competencies necessary for effective change managers. Effective change managers will have a good understanding of group dynamics processes because so much of their time will be spent working with teams responsible for rollout or communication. A change manager must also have good process consultation skills, because he or she needs to be good at observing both individuals and groups, seeing how they interact, and knowing how their interactions affect others. In addition, change managers need to have good facilitation skills because they may be responsible for planning or facilitating meetings, feedback sessions, and organizational conversations about the intervention. Consequently, individuals with strong OD consulting backgrounds can make effective change managers.

Noted

Of the four performance consultant roles, the one of change manager is least likely to exist as an independent position. Chances are that as a performance consultant you'll be asked to assume this role in addition to one of the other three roles (analyst, intervention specialist, or evaluator). Change managers generally deal with two different types of challenges: getting buy-in (or overcoming resistance) and addressing implementation issues of large projects.

Evaluator

The fourth role that performance consultants may play is that of evaluator (Rothwell, 1999). The evaluator is responsible for measuring results on a variety of levels. For instance, the evaluator may be asked to assess the degree to which participants have improved their skills, or the evaluator may need to identify how much impact the solution had on larger business goals (such as increasing sales or improving market share or enhancing customer responsiveness).

Basic Rule 10

The evaluator is responsible for measurement—especially of solutions and their impact on the organization.

Ideally, the evaluator is involved in the performance consulting process from the very beginning so that the initial client conversations about the objectives of the consulting work, the importance of the performance gap, and the purpose and goals of the performers are all clearly understood. All of these pieces are critical when it comes to determining the evaluation strategy and metrics for measurement.

Additionally, the evaluator needs to discuss with the client the resources—time and money—required for the intervention and its evaluation. However, often an evaluator is brought into a project after a solution has been implemented when the customer is pressured to show the value of the work. In these cases (where the evaluator was not on hand for the early conversations to shape expectations and identify appropriate targets), the evaluation process is reactive. The evaluator may also be brought in to help improve particular interventions during the piloting or beta-test stages.

Noted

It is rare for performance consultants to play only one of these four roles. It is more likely that a performance consultant wears several hats and bears responsibility for the roles of analyst, evaluator, change manager, and, on occasion, intervention specialist. In smaller organizations, the performance consultant is responsible for all four roles.

Evaluators must have several basic competencies. In fact, many of the skills such as data gathering and analytical skills that are important for analysts are also very useful for evaluators. Evaluators need the ability to compare results to organizational goals. Also, evaluators must have standard-setting skills, which are used to measure desired results and to help others establish targets. Effective feedback skills is another basic competency that an evaluator must have, because he or she will be reporting results back to clients and stakeholders and may often be delivering bad news.

Noted

Evaluators, because of their data-gathering expertise, may often be used to design and conduct organization-wide surveys or culture audits. Although not strictly evaluations of interventions (these more typically fall into assessments), these surveys do tap into the expertise of evaluators. Also, evaluators may also be brought in to provide unbiased assessment of the success or failure of a project conducted by another consultant. This is a means of ensuring an independent and objective assessment instead of asking the original consultant to evaluate his or her own project.

How HPI Differs From Your Current Work

It's possible that the nature of performance consultant work and approach bears a tremendous resemblance to your current role. However, it's more likely that HPI constitutes a wide range of changes for you. Robinson and Robinson (1996) present a wide-ranging list of some differences between HPI work and the more traditional training and OD functions. It is useful to be familiar with these differences because you may need to explain to others (such as trainers, your manager, clients, or OD consultants) how the nature of your work has changed and why HPI is different from other approaches or your previous role.

Focus

Although the traditional trainer may think about the business and certainly want it to succeed, the trainer's focus is on learning activities—and producing training that addresses the learning needs of people. The performance consultant's focus is on the business goals and what prevents the organization from meeting those targets.

Noted

Don't assume HPI is just something to add on to a traditional HR structure as if it were another new service (like a new training class or additional facilitation skills). Likewise, becoming a performance consultant isn't just about having some new tools in your toolbox. HPI means approaching client requests and problems differently.

Output

Trainers are accountable for effective learning experiences. OD practitioners are accountable for the interventions they design. But, performance consultants share responsibility for changing organizational results. This is a much higher level of accountability than that of a traditional trainer or even an OD consultant.

Partnering

Performance consultants likely do almost all of their work in collaboration with clients. This is because most of the resources necessary to complete the performance work (such as access to data, exemplary performers, and resources) are owned by the client and not the performance consultant. Additionally, the performance consultant is likely to find that a client's problems are caused by an element outside the client's department (such as another department), so the performance consultant can't always count on the client to resolve key resource or implementation issues.

Activities

Too often, people think that performance consulting is like being a trainer except it involves doing more interventions than training. Not true. Some performance consultants don't do any training at all. Other performance consultants end up delivering mostly knowledge and skills solutions.

Whether you're considered a performance consultant isn't determined by what solutions you implement, it's determined by the process you use to identify those solutions. However, what you're likely to find as a performance consultant is that you spend more time gathering and analyzing information and less time actually delivering solutions (such as leading a training class or facilitating a team-building session). It's much easier to find a good trainer, instructional designer, facilitator, or OD consultant than it is to find a good performance consultant. Consequently, your time will become more valuable, and you will need to delegate or outsource functions that can be performed by others.

The HPI Process

You've had a chance to examine a definition of performance consulting, look at what HPI is and isn't, note the key performance roles, and see differences between HPI and traditional training roles. HPI relies upon the basic process depicted in figure 2-1. Although several different models are used to depict performance, the HPI process is fairly consistent regardless of the practitioner or organization.

The HPI process starts with a business analysis. In this stage, the performance consultant partners with the client to identify the major organizational priorities and the performance that is critical if those priorities are to be achieved. The critical performance is then reviewed for performance gaps, and the consultant identifies the causes of those gaps. At this point, the performance consultant can make intervention recommendations to the client. The decisions by the client lead to implementation of particular performance initiatives. The performance consultant seeks to improve the intervention during implementation with formative evaluation and then conducts a summative evaluation to determine the impact on the organization. Throughout the entire process, the performance consultant deals with change management issues. This is only an abbreviated explanation of the HPI process. The elements of this process will be explored in more detail in the chapters to follow.

Getting It Done

This chapter covered what performance consulting or HPI is. It's important to understand what performance consulting is and is not. These distinctions help clarify what it means to be a performance consultant and the practical changes it will mean for you as you make the transition to HPI work. What you've learned here will not only help clarify this issue in your mind, but also will help you deal with discussions with others (such as managers, peers, or potential clients) when you have to explain what a performance consultant is. The questions posed in exercise 2-1 can help you apply the content from this chapter to your own work circumstances.

Figure 2-1. The HPI model.

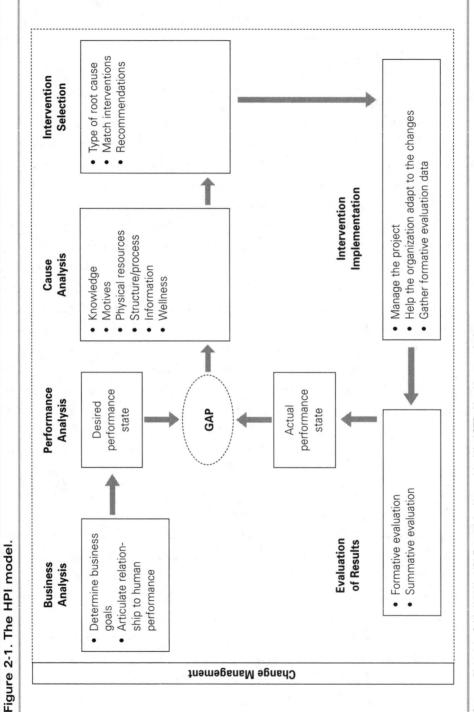

Source: Piskurich, G.M. (2002). *HPI Essentials*. Alexandria, VA: ASTD. Used by permission.

Exercise 2-1. Where do you fit into the role of performance consulting?

1. What other functions (such as OD, quality, Six Sigma, HR, strategic planning) within your organization may perceive you as a rival? How can you clarify the differences between what they do and what HPI is to them? How can you enlist them to work with you to solve performance issues?

2. How will your current role change as you move into performance consulting?

3. Which performance consulting role (analyst, intervention specialist, change manager, evaluator) do you have the most interest in?

4. How will you explain to potential clients what it is that performance consultants do?

5. What confusion is there around performance within your organization or client base? How could this create problems or challenges for you?

This chapter focused on providing background and foundational material. Subsequent chapters hone in on practical tips for performance consulting work.

In the next chapter, you'll look at the performance consulting process by understanding the element of business focus and the process of dealing with business goals. This element of the HPI process is one of the aspects that differentiates the HPI process from the way that most HR professionals work.

3

Human Performance Improvement Is Business Focused

What's Inside This Chapter

Here you'll see how to:

▶ Conduct a front-end analysis
▶ Define the term *business focus* in terms of performance
▶ Avoid common mistakes performance consultants make that prevent their work from being business focused
▶ Develop strategies for moving clients to a business-focused approach from a transactional approach
▶ Become a more effective performance consultant through partnering.

What Does Business Focused Mean?

Being business focused means that one is clear about what the organization's strategic priorities are and uses those priorities to guide decisions about what to focus on. It isn't enough to do something because a client requests it or because there is a performance gap. In any organization there are always lots of things that are broken or could be improved, but that doesn't mean that improving that specific performance or repairing that broken process will contribute much to the organization and key business goals. Therefore, the process of analyzing performance always begins with business analysis, which allows performance consultants to be business focused.

Being business focused also means determining what key organizational goals are not being met because of a particular performance gap. Only then is it justified to pursue closing that gap. Otherwise, consultants can invest time and valuable resources to close a performance gap that ends up having no meaningful impact on the organization. Thus, HPI starts by determining what matters to the organization—what the key goals are—and helping the organization achieve those goals.

Think About This

Most organizations and managers assume that the business goals are clear. This assumption often is wrong. Most workers have trouble identifying what the specific targets are for the business and what accomplishments they produce that drive those goals. Sometimes what managers claim to be organizational priorities are actually outdated. Never take for granted what the client says in terms of business goals, but always look for ways to verify those claims.

So, how does a performance consultant start the process with a business focus? A business-focused approach to client requests requires the performance consultant to start the analysis by identifying what the key business goals are for the client or organization. For instance, if a client requests time management training because he or she thinks the staff is inefficient, the performance consultant must turn the conversation to the goals or objectives that the client's team or department is accountable for. Once the performance consultant determines what those critical priorities are, the performance consultant can then work backward from that point to identify the staff performance necessary to achieve those business goals.

When you focus on business goals, it could mean goals for the entire organization, a department, a team, a unit, or a function. As a performance consultant, you should focus on the goals that provide a balance between importance, measurability, and linkage to the issue the client is concerned with.

For instance, if the director of recruiting in a power plant is concerned about the efficiency of the support staff within the recruiting office, there are business goals at different levels. The company's business goal might be to increase the generating capacity by 2 percent in the next quarter. However, there may be a number of steps between increasing possible efficiency of HR recruiting administrative staff and electrical capacity. The business goal for the recruiting office itself might be to fill all vacancies within four weeks or less. That business goal is probably affected significantly by the efficiency of the administrative staff. Consequently, it's probably a better business goal to focus on.

Basic Rule 11

In a large and complex organization, there are usually a variety of business goals at different levels of the organization. Work with the client to identify the business goals that appear to be the best fit for the problem that the client wants to focus on.

Tackling performance issues with a business focus is critical. It makes it much easier to identify the critical performance gaps (and also to avoid spending time on performance gaps that don't matter very much to the organization). A business focus also makes evaluation and calculating the ROI of the eventual solutions much easier to determine. When the business analysis step is skipped or done poorly, then the evaluation aspect of the process usually takes much longer and the risk of choosing the wrong intervention (and thus failing) is greater.

Front-End Analysis—An Overview

Throughout this book, you'll look at specific pieces of front-end analysis, but it's helpful to take a general overview to understand better how specific elements are integrated.

Front-end analysis is the process of identifying business goals, determining what performance is critical to achieve those goals, determining which performance outcomes have significant gaps, and then figuring out what the causes of those gaps are.

Think About This

There is a tendency to assume that whatever the client wants is important to the business because the client knows what the organizational priorities are. Plus, being responsive is a hallmark of good customer service. No matter how insistent the client, performance consultants need to rein in the tendency to respond in knee-jerk fashion to any problem the client raises. Regardless of the request, an effective performance consultant needs to go back to the business goals and then see how that performance is relevant to those goals. Keeping clients happy is not the same as generating business results.

It is a subset of the HPI process. From the client's perspective, the front-end analysis (sometimes referred to as a "front-end" or FEA) is one piece of work or one service leading to a series of outputs (recommendations for solutions to performance gaps). From the performance consultant's perspective, the front-end analysis is a series of stages or steps (see figure 3-1).

As the model shows, worker performance is generated by having influences (environment and support) that allow the appropriate tasks (behaviors) and processes to generate outcomes (accomplishments) that lead to organizational results. However, the front-end analysis begins at the other end of this process by starting with the business goals, then determining what performance outcomes are critical drivers, which drivers have gaps, and the causes of those gaps.

Basic Rule 12

Individual performance builds to generate business results, but performance analysis starts on the opposite end (business analysis) to provide objectivity and ensure that the right priorities are focused on.

Identifying Business Goals Is Critical

Because front-end analysis starts with determining the business goal, it's critical to get clients to provide their organizational priorities. Difficulties arise when some clients don't know what the key priorities are for their organization or their priorities have

Figure 3-1. A model of front-end analysis.

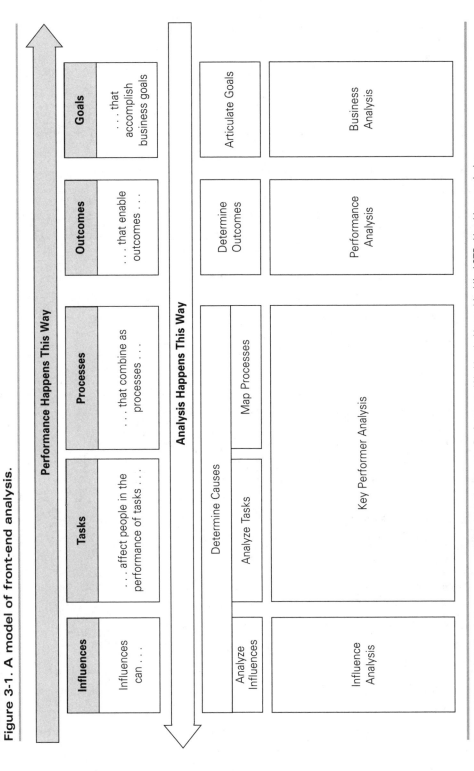

Source: ASTD and Platinum Performance. (2004). *Analyzing Human Performance Workbook*. Alexandria, VA: ASTD. Used by permission.

become outdated. In addition, clients might provide strategic goals that are still too general to serve the HPI process.

For example, a client might claim that the highest priority is to increase sales. A good performance consultant will push for more details and information regarding this goal by asking questions. How much of an increase in sales? When does that increase need to happen? Is the sales increase to be overall or to a specific part of the market (such as new customers)? Does it matter what mix of products is sold to achieve that increase? Is increased sales being measured by total number of sales or income?

Therefore, when clients say the goal is to increase sales, it's important to push, prod, and coach for enough details so the business goal is specific and tied to a time-frame. The goal of increasing sales, for example, should eventually end up as a variation that sounds something like increasing sales of existing products by 2 percent by the end of this fiscal year. What's important to note about this goal is that when stated this way, the business goal has targets. There is a number to hit and a time to hit it by, and it sounds like something the organization already measures (which will make evaluation easier).

Think About This

If clients aren't clear about their business goals, one technique to get clarity is to ask the question, "What would success look like for this team or office?" Other alternatives include: "What would this team have to do for you to get promoted?" or "How does the organization define what a good year looks like for this office?" or "How does your manager decide if this department has performed very well?"

It's important to verify that it is a realistic organizational target. Sometimes clients, when pressed for specifics, just pull numbers out of thin air ("I'd like to increase our customer satisfaction scores by, um . . .40 percent, yeah, 40 percent . . . in the next year, er . . . no, in the next quarter"). If it seems that the targets established by the client aren't realistic or haven't been thought through, then it's critical to help them develop more accurate targets. This book offers more details later about how to go about doing this.

Basic Rule 13

The business goal for the client ideally should be quantitative and time bound, and it needs to be a legitimate focus of the business.

Additionally, clients may be convinced that something is the real business goal when they've really only stated a possible way to meet a goal. These are instances where the goal stated by the clients actually implies or assumes other targets.

Let's examine the example of employee morale (a common issue for many organizations). Plenty of organizations do an organizational climate study, a culture audit, or an employee survey and discover that employee morale is low. Senior management is then mobilized to do something about "the morale problem," and that's when someone usually gets called into the office of the vice president of human resources to find out that the new high-priority assignment is to improve company morale.

The problem with this example is that most organizations that decide that improving morale is important don't do so because improving morale is a real company goal. It's absolutely legitimate for a CEO to conclude that one of the organization's top four goals is to improve employee morale. In such an instance, it's understandable when the business wants to improve morale and expects no other results from this. However, in most cases, organizations seeking to improve morale are usually trying to achieve something else. According to management's thinking, if morale improves, then maybe turnover will go down or perhaps a more positive atmosphere would improve customer service. In addition, seeking to improve morale is often an attempt to increase the quality and creativity of employees' work.

In short, the client may claim the goal is to improve morale but has other intentions and is guilty of assuming that morale is the key to that happening. But, what's tricky about these situations is that the client may not know what the real goal is. Thus, the client may pursue an improvement in morale without understanding that the real objective is something else. That is why so many organizations that get internal audits showing low morale are galvanized to do something; they assume that morale is responsible for producing some other business result. Morale can play an important role in various business results, or it can prove to be mostly irrelevant in the outcomes the organization achieves. It's important not to confuse the *means* of

Think About This

If the client identifies a business goal that seems to be much closer to the means of an unstated goal, press the client on what is supposed to happen if that goal is achieved. If the client is looking for a result from that goal, then the performance consultant will need to find out what the unstated result is that the client expects from the means. One way to identify if the claimed goal is a true business goal is to ask the client, "If we increased morale and nothing else came from this—no other improvements or benefits to the organization—would you be OK with that?" Something is a legitimate business goal if the client is willing to accept that nothing else may happen as a result of achieving the goal.

achieving a goal (in this case, seeking to improve morale) with the *goal itself* (what management hopes to get as a result when morale improves).

When a client engages in this kind of thinking ("The goal is to improve morale, but what I really want is to see happen is improved retention"), then the process is not business focused. Instead of focusing on a business goal (improving retention), the organization is making an assumption about the nature of the solution ("We'll improve retention by improving morale").

Incorrect assumptions create problems for the HPI process. There are plenty of cases of workforces with poor morale that performed well (or had good retention), and those with good morale that performed poorly (or still had high turnover). The point is not that morale is irrelevant to retention; it's that morale is not always (and usually rarely) the most important force affecting retention or other goals.

Noted

Ideally, business goals are time bound and quantitative, but many legitimate organizational priorities fail that test. The key is not to only accept goals with numbers and dates, but to confirm that the goals as stated are truly goals of the business and that the organization isn't deceiving itself about what its real objectives are.

How can performance consultants determine if the goal provided by the client is a legitimate business goal? One option is to push the client to see if the goal from the client is really the end result sought by the organization. Such goals as improving the quality of work life, boosting morale, or having more fun by decreasing stress are likely to be focused on the client, not the company.

For instance, if the client has a goal of "be listed as one of 'Working Mother's Top 100 Firms to Work for,'" then it's important to know why that goal matters to the client. If the client provides an answer like "So I can improve retention" or "So we can do a better job recruiting women," then the original statement was not the true goal. That's because the client is stating something as a goal that is really a means to get somewhere else (the real goal, in this case, increased retention or improved recruitment). But, if the client's answer is "I don't want to work anyplace where people aren't treated well," then the goal of making the list of top firms to work for is a legitimate business goal.

Think About This

When a client claims something to be a goal, the performance consultant should ask, "And that is important because . . .?" If the client relates it to corporate values by saying, "It's important for us to treat our people right" or "We have an ethical contract with our staff to treat them with respect and dignity," then it's a real business objective. However, if the client talks about the benefits of this goal—by how it leads to something else, then the client is guilty of assuming that a solution category is the business goal.

Why Clients Lose Their Business Focus

As senior managers insist that all units of the organization place more emphasis on key goals and focus on the bottom line, it's common for training managers to talk about being more strategic and "having a seat at the table." Most professionals at least pay lip service to how important it is to let the organization's priorities be their drivers—to determine what should be focused on.

Unfortunately, most people in the organization (and that definitely includes trainers, OD professionals, HR, line managers, and department directors) become so busy that they lose sight of what is really critical to the organization. Additionally, despite the best of intentions, it is easy to eventually evolve into organizational silos where work becomes narrowly focused and performers are less aware of the big picture. As performance leader Geary Rummler has noted, as organizations grow, processes break down with greater frequency (Rummler & Brache, 1990). This is because as the organization gets bigger, all processes—from performance management to service recovery to building security to recruitment—involve more players and become more convoluted. It becomes harder for participants in the process to see their effect on the end result. Individuals see only their one little piece of the puzzle, often leading to well-meaning managers working against each other because processes have evolved that cut against each other or are inconsistent.

One example is an organization that shifts to team structures and continues to place emphasis on an appraisal system that is individually based (and therefore rewards people for individual performance, not team-based success). Another case is an organization where recruiting seeks to fill positions quicker by loosening employment standards while security causes delays in filling positions by rigorously enforcing background check requirements.

For all of these reasons, clients usually aren't focused on critical business objectives when they request a particular intervention. Hence, very reasonable and competent professionals often insist that what they are requesting is for the good of the business; yet they lack a real understanding of the organizational priorities, and their request (for a specific intervention) isn't driven by business needs.

Basic Rule 14

The larger the organization or more complex the work processes, the more likely it is that performers and clients have lost sight of organizational priorities.

Identify Key Performance Drivers

Let's suppose that the client has identified the real business objectives for the department or organization. The performance consultant has confirmed that those are indeed the goals of the business (or goals of a department that supports the larger organization's objectives). Furthermore, the performance consultant has worked with the client to make sure the business goals are described in a measurable and time-bound manner. Does that mean the business analysis stage of the performance consulting process is over? No—the performance consultant still has one more part to ensure a business focus.

It is important to identify the important accomplishments or performance that drives the relevant business goals. For instance, if the business goal is to increase sales by 10 percent in the next quarter, the critical performance drivers necessary to achieve that goal might consist of 1) a close rate of 32 percent for all sales, 2) customer retention of 78 percent or better, and 3) increased pool of new customers by at least 30 percent (assuming a retention rate of 78 percent of existing customers). Those three accomplishments are the three critical performance accomplishments that will determine whether or not the firm can increase sales by 10 percent in the next quarter. To put it another way, the business goal is what the organization wants to get, and the performance drivers are the accomplishments that have to occur if the goal is going to be achieved. Although many things can affect whether the business goal is achieved, the key drivers are those performance factors that are the most critical—have the most impact—on achieving the goal.

Basic Rule 15

After the performance consultant has established what the business goals are, it's important to determine what performance is critical to those goals. All types of performance may affect a goal but the performance consultant must determine what is incidental or minimal versus what really serves as a driver for that business objective.

To determine the performance drivers—the accomplishments critical for the business goal—the performance consultant begins with the business goal. If the performance consultant starts by looking at the intervention that the client suggests, it would be possible to rationalize how almost any solution can contribute to any goal. The result would then be an intervention that has little or no impact on the business.

By starting with the business goal in mind, the performance consultant can then sort out what performance is critical versus what performance has little impact. There may be hundreds of different performance areas that contribute to the business goal. Just because there is a performance gap doesn't mean it's worth closing that gap. The best value to the organization is to focus on performance gaps that make a difference—

performance that determines whether or not the organization will hit important business objectives. The only way to achieve that is by focusing on key drivers for that performance rather than on any performance area that is not optimized.

Noted

Many different types of performance may have some impact on whether or not the organization reaches a business goal, but it's important to be focused on the primary performance drivers for that business goal. Otherwise, all the time and resources spent to improve performance may improve performance in that specific area a lot but have minimal or no business impact.

How can performance consultants identify the accomplishments that are critical to the business goal? Several options are available. Although clients may lose sight of what performance gap should be a priority, they may understand and can explain what performance drives key goals. If they don't know that information, then interviews with the top performers in the organization are usually revealing. These star performers can provide insights about accomplishments that are critical to achieve a particular goal.

Observation is another powerful method to identify key performance, because it enables you to see how one performer (who is very successful at one particular accomplishment) has better results than another performer. Many organizations have made the effort to try to identify what the core competencies are within their industry (thus leading to the outsourcing of elements that don't play a critical role in achieving business goals). This is similar to the process necessary here. The actual process starts with determining which accomplishments are critical to achieving a business goal. The way to do this is by starting with the business goal and working backward, rather than starting with an intervention and justifying why it has value to the organization.

Here is an example of this process in action: Your client, the director of sales, requests time management training for the administrative staff in the sales department. When asked why the time management training is important, the client argues that if the administrative staff is more efficient, they'll get more work done. This would mean better support for the salesforce, which would result in or

Basic Rule 16

Always start with the business goal and work backward to identify the performance critical in achieving that goal, determine what gaps exist in that performance, and then determine the causes of those gaps.

contribute to increased sales of 10 percent for this quarter (which, coincidently, is the objective for the sales department).

This sounds plausible, doesn't it? And, you've probably heard plenty of analyses similar to that. Unfortunately, it's probably wrong. Start with the business goal and then determine what the key performance is that affects sales. It is likely that the administrative staff contributes to the sales success to some degree, but realistically, such issues as the salesforce's closing skills, customer retention, and the number of sales calls are all likely to have far greater impact than the ability of the administrative staff to quickly process records.

What this example shows is that starting with the solution the client wants leads to rationalizing the value. Starting with the business goals first and then asking what the performance is that has the most impact on the business goals leads to the performance gaps worth addressing. In this instance, if close rate, customer retention rate, and number of sales calls were the three most important accomplishments for meeting the department's quarterly goal, then focusing on administrative staff time management likely will have no impact on that goal.

Some Myths Around Business Analysis

Human resource development professionals are prone to make several errors regarding business focus and business analysis.

We Don't Have Business Goals Because We're Not a Business. This statement is nonsensical. Even if the company is nonprofit or government-based, the word *business* in the context of this chapter refers to an enterprise or organization. All organizations exist for a purpose. That purpose means that the organization establishes goals to help it fulfill that purpose. Maybe the employees aren't unified around that purpose or possibly the goals are fuzzy, outdated, or in conflict with other business goals. No matter what the circumstances, all organizations have critical goals.

Many of the examples in this book revolve around sales because that's usually a simple concept to explain and understand. But, even organizations that don't measure success by sales or market share have other measures. For instance, other business goals for departments or offices might revolve around:

- cycle time (how quickly work is done)
- rework (amount of mistakes or material wasted)
- customer service satisfaction (keep the customers coming back)
- budget and productivity (getting the same amount of work done for less money)
- accuracy or quality (reports with better focus)
- robustness (a solution or system or process that is less likely to break down and has more resiliency).

Practically all organizations and their subunits have expectations for what success looks like. Those standards of success are business goals.

Think About This

If the client has a problem with the term *business goal,* then try using an alternative phrase. Some substitutes might be *organizational priorities, strategic imperatives, department targets, unit goals, year-end numbers, objectives,* or *measures of success.*

A superficial analysis of the business objectives means that the performance process is not business focused. If the client gets away with specifying something that isn't truly a goal but rather a tenuous means to another goal, then the performance work will not be business focused. If client goals aren't specific or easily measurable, then evaluation becomes difficult. In addition, if client goals are arbitrary, then it isn't a true business goal because it isn't clear if the client's stated goal is a real objective or something that was a whim of the moment.

Some Things Just Can't Be Measured. Evaluation is covered in more detail later in the book, but it's appropriate to cover some measurement issues at this point. There

Think About This

Never let the client argue that the business goal is obvious so it isn't necessary to determine it. If the link between business goal and performance is clear and obvious, then identifying the business goal won't take much effort. If the client resists on this issue, it's a reason to push back even harder.

is a tendency from some trainers to argue that a range of things just can't be measured (and thus it isn't possible to come up with quantitative business goals for that target). It's common to argue that soft-skills training can't be measured; however, this is a fallacy. Following the HPI process makes almost anything measurable.

Think About This

Almost everything is measurable. Things are difficult to measure when the business goal is unclear and evaluation isn't discussed until the end of the work. If the client insists that the goal can't be measured, ask the client what the result of the goal will be. That outcome or result almost always is measurable.

The Client's Requested Solution Is the Place to Start. If the client asks for team building, it's easy to rationalize how team building might lead to a particular level of performance and a rationalization about how that particular performance is vital to a key organizational goal. That is exactly how most open-enrollment training is justified in organizations, yet this approach has repeatedly been shown to be fallacious.

It's critical to start with the business goal, identify the key performance drivers, and then look for performance gaps. Only after these steps have been taken is it possible to move to determining what the solution should be—and be confident that the solution will have some impact on the business.

Noted

It's always possible to find a way to link a behavior or a proposed intervention to some major business goal focusing on the behavior or intervention. But by starting the analysis with the business goal, the performance that plays a minor role to that goal is weeded out, and that allows a more objective analysis. The order of the analysis is crucial with this work in order to be successful.

Getting the Client to Be Business Focused

One possible challenge with being business focused is that it is not usually where the client starts. Typically, a client will approach with a specific intervention in mind. The client seeks agreement to provide communication skills training or a team-building intervention or some other hypothetical solution. Any conversation with the client needs to start where the client is mentally and that will almost always be at the transactional or solution level.

Once the conversation has approached what the client wants to do, it's time to shift the conversation to more strategic levels. Ask the client what kinds of goals the performers in question are accountable for. Once it's clear what those key goals are, it's possible to work backward and determine what performance is critical to those goals.

Oftentimes, as the performance consultant moves from the business goal to the performance drivers, the client will recognize that choosing the intervention now is premature—that he or she has asked for something (such as communication skills

Think About This

A very easy way to segue from a discussion on a specific intervention (such as supervisory skills training) to key business goals is to ask, "I need some background about these performers. What kind of results do they need to generate? What outcomes are they responsible for?" This won't look like a shift in the conversation but tends to come off as a request for useful background information.

training) before all the facts were accounted for. The client may also realize that the requested solution has no relevance to the business goal and critical performance.

Sometimes the performance consultant asks the client what performance is critical for the business goal and the client won't know. That is the cue to ask, "Would you like me to find out?" This gives the performance consultant the support needed to do the kind of information gathering that leads to real performance improvement. But, in any of these situations, the interaction from the client will have shifted from a transactional one (providing a specific service—such as a particular training class or OD intervention) to a performance-focused one.

Think About This

If the client can't answer what the key drivers or performances are necessary to achieve the key business goal, always ask, "Would you like me to find out?" This shifts the conversation from a focus on fulfilling a request (providing specific training) to being strategic, focusing on performance results, and clarifying priorities.

Partnering Is Critical

One adjustment needed when switching from training to performance consulting is partnering. Partnering does not come naturally for trainers. When clients come to a trainer, the trainer tends to own the training resources. Although some negotiation goes back and forth with the client about such issues as the length of the training, the content, and the target audience, it's the trainer who owns the training function and the development of any training.

The vast majority of the time, the key issues, resources, and performers fall outside the authority of the performance consultant, and, therefore, he or she needs to get cooperation from clients. Therefore, a performance consultant requires partnering for almost all work.

Basic Rule 17

Performance consultants must work in partnerships if they are to be effective.

Continuing to take and fulfill orders is incompatible with performance consulting. Instead, it is critical to work with clients and performers to design collaborative approaches. Consequently, the ability to work well with others is a critical skill for effective performance consulting. It's necessary to identify key players (such as people to whom the client reports, those who own key resources that the performance consultant needs to access, union representatives, and whomever the top performers report to) and work with them.

Noted

Effective partnering requires the ability to negotiate expectations and roles upfront with the client. In addition, good diplomacy to build alliances and gain access to important resources is critical. Finally, insight into change management issues aids the partnering issue.

Think About This

In the initial client meetings, a good way to manage client expectations is to cover the seven *R*s:

- **Results:** What are the business objectives that matter, and what drives those goals?
- **Relationship:** What kind of interaction do you need from the client during the project?
- **Roadmap:** What is the process and approximate timeline for the initial work?
- **Roles:** Where and when is the client involved in the front-end analysis work?
- **Responsibilities:** Who is accountable for what in this process?
- **Reporting requirements:** Is the information confidential? How often does the client need to hear from you and in what format?
- **Results:** What outcomes or business goals are sought or expected after all the work is done?

Some of the partnering work occurs with the initial client contact. During that time, it's critical to manage expectations and help guide the client in the right direction (away from instant solutions and toward an HPI approach). It's also necessary to identify if the performance consulting work involves diagnostic analysis (dealing with poor performance) or new performance planning (current performance is fine but the client wants improvement, perhaps because goals are being raised or new types of work will be done).

Partnering continues throughout the performance consulting process. It is important to partner during the intervention design phase, pulling in key resources from other departments (subject matter experts or support from the OD, Six Sigma, or quality office). Partnering is also critical during the roll-out effort, which likely will include a communication plan and a series of ways for reaching out to participants of projects that involve large numbers of performers).

Getting It Done

Chapter 3 demonstrated how critical the business goal phase is to successful HPI work. Exercise 3-1 gives you the opportunity to apply what you learned and identify areas for improvement.

Exercise 3-1. Identifying business goals.

1. What skills or knowledge do you need to acquire to improve your ability to understand and discuss business goals with potential clients? Do you need more background in reading spreadsheets and profit-loss information? Are you comfortable reading an annual report or shareholder's analysis?

2. There is almost always business analysis information about your organization you can acquire proactively. What kinds of information (such as strategic plans, core value statements, and departmental objectives) are available to you? Where could you go to get this kind of information?

(continued on page 50)

Exercise 3-1. Identifying business goals (continued).

3. When a client provides you with what is claimed to be a business goal for the client's department, where can you go to confirm that this is an accurate business objective? Are there other stakeholders or organizational documents that can verify this as a business goal?

4. Identify an open-enrollment course available to a client that appears to have some relevance to the client (such as a conflict management course that is supposed to improve the ability of staff to work together, thus improving productivity by reducing unnecessary conflict and bickering). Have the course providers been able to demonstrate any impact on key organizational goals because of this course? Then, identify the primary business objectives of this client. Working backward, determine what performance is critical to achieving these objectives. Does this open-enrollment course appear to have any clear connection to any of these objectives?

In the next chapter, you'll learn how to identify performance gaps in areas that are critical to achieving key business goals.

4
Performance Consulting Focuses on Accomplishments

What's Inside This Chapter

Here you'll see how to:

- ▶ Distinguish between accomplishments and behaviors
- ▶ Use accomplishments to assess performance gaps
- ▶ Identify or develop accomplishments or outcomes
- ▶ Find and analyze exemplars to discover what makes them so successful
- ▶ Eschew common mistakes consultants make about performance outcomes.

Accomplishment Versus Behavior

One significant difference between performance consulting and other HRD approaches is the distinction between accomplishment and behavior—a critical difference for performance consultants (Gilbert, 1996).

Most people are taught to focus on behavior when evaluating performance. At work, performance appraisals tend to emphasize what people do and the skills they possess (activities and competencies). First-time employees learn quickly how critical it is to look busy when management is around. Position descriptions and job ads usually delineate work in terms of what activities people will do or the attributes expected of them (table 4-1). The following job listing is typical of many of the position descriptions listed on online job banks for trainers: "Design and update curriculum and deliver training to both new hires and existing staff. Deliver training to end users, department trainers, and others as deemed necessary. Design and develop a quality monitoring program to evaluate agent success toward those key drivers. Identify training needs for the organization, and develop or modify the curriculum to address those needs." Do you notice how much of the position description talks about the activities the person in this job would do?

Table 4-1. Measuring performance through behavior versus accomplishments.

Profession	Behavior	Accomplishment/Outcome
Airplane Pilot	Completes takeoff checklist, contacts tower	Safe takeoff from runway
Accountant	Follows procedure, reviews financial records	Accurate, on-time financial report
Trainer	Conducts ice-breaker activity, debriefs activities, answers questions, delivers material	Knowledgeable participants
Editor	Reviews submissions, decides editorial direction, selects topics	Profitable, informative, polished magazine

Check out your own résumé. It's likely to be written in terms of behavior and competencies—what you do and what you know. The key point, though, is that none of these examples focused on accomplishments or outcomes. Generally speaking, organizations talk about the importance of performance but then seek to focus on behavior and skills.

This focus on behaviors is typical of how most organizations manage work. Managers continually seek to punish or reward particular kinds of behavior. But, measuring behavior is especially subjective. Generally speaking, it's difficult to evaluate behavior without actually watching or seeing the behavior. Additionally, even

Noted

Behavior is not the end that the business seeks. The point is that the organization doesn't care about hustle if the work doesn't get done. Managers don't care if employees know how to do the work if they can't get it done correctly. Behavior is important for the most part because it should result in accomplishments.

when managers observe behavior, it's not possible to watch the performer constantly because managers have too much to do. Consequently, small snapshots of employee behavior are no guarantee that the performer behaves that way constantly. Because people act differently when they know they're being observed by others (especially management), judging performance on the basis of behavior is very subjective. Managers who focus on behavior as a means of evaluating performance are relying on subjective measures. As a result, many performers tend to perceive such managers as playing favorites or being biased (because the performer perceives the behavior in a different fashion).

Noted

Trying to assess behavior is very difficult and tends to be subjective. For example, how can you measure "hustle"? What metrics are there for "responsive to customer needs" or "demonstrates initiative"? By looking at what those behaviors are supposed to produce, however, it is easier to identify appropriate measures. For instance, "hustle" is important in order to have "short lines" or "completed assignments." Good customer service skills (such as "responsive to customer needs") result in "customer retention" or "satisfied customers."

Basic Rule 18

Performance consulting primarily focuses on accomplishments and outcomes instead of behaviors.

HPI focuses on accomplishments before considering behavior. It is important to be clear on what this means. First, an accomplishment or outcome is something that is of value to the organization. For example, if a performer is entering records into a database, what the organization wants from this is an accurate, up-to-date database on or before the assigned deadline. It is probably of no value to the organization if the performer hustles, smiles while entering the data, tries really hard, or inputs the data creatively if the data isn't accurate, current, and finished by the deadline. In short, behaving well usually doesn't matter if the performer doesn't produce the results the organization wants.

Remember, an accomplishment is what is of value to the organization. Now, if the hypothetical database worker has to perform the database work in an office accessible to the public (where customers are), then perhaps smiling and behaving in an outgoing manner are important to the organization. In this case, the outcome the performer is responsible for is "producing an accurate, up-to-date database by the deadline in a customer-friendly manner."

Basic Rule 19

HPI defines an accomplishment or outcome as something that is of value to the organization.

Noted

An accomplishment or outcome usually is a result. Sometimes an accomplishment can also involve how the work is done. If it is critical that performers use a particular process or method for achieving a result, then that process would be part of the outcome. An example of an accomplishment for a chief financial officer would be maintaining balanced financial records using generally accepted accounting principles.

There are many reasons to start with accomplishments or outcomes when looking at performance. Accomplishments are much easier to measure than behavior because behavior requires subjective measurement unlike accomplishments. Two performers can have almost identical behavior but radically different results, because one of the performers might accidentally omit a key step. Thomas Gilbert has developed a number of examples in his work to demonstrate this point (Gilbert, 1996). A similar example is shown in table 4-2. Finally, focusing on accomplishments is fairer and recognizes individual differences.

How is focusing on accomplishments fairer and more appropriate for individual behavior? Look at the act of writing reports. Luis may be very organized when he writes a report assignment. He gathers data, generates an outline, does three draft

Table 4-2. Almost identical behavior, yet different results.

Smith and Jones are candidates for an administrative position in your company. You decide to run them through a battery of tests to see who would be the better performer. Here are the results:

Test of Performance	Smith	Jones
Knowledge and skills using a PC and word processing software	99 out of 100	99 out of 100
Completed and accurate reports with no typos	0% completed	5 completed (out of 5) for 100%
Customer service skills and behavior with callers	99 out of 100	99 out of 100
Satisfied customers	0% satisfied	90% satisfied

If you look at behavior, Smith and Jones are identical with PC and word processing knowledge and skills and behavior; they sound like carbon copies of each other. But if you look at accomplishments, Jones scores 100 percent (she completed all of her reports of sufficient quality and on time) while Smith completed none of his reports. How can this be? Smith is missing one key behavior: He never saves any of his documents. Looking at customer service skills and behavior—again, Smith and Jones appear identical. But, Smith leaves a trail of angry callers because every time he attempts to transfer the call he disconnects them. The only behavior Smith is deficient on is transferring the call in which he appears incapable of doing so effectively. By comparison, Jones sometimes fails to mention the organization's name when answering the phone, but most of her callers are satisfied.

If you judge by behavior, Smith and Jones are two peas in a pod. If you judge by accomplishments, Smith is a failure and Jones a fine performer. Smith fails at critical behaviors. So, it's hard to judge performance on the basis of behavior (especially since managers almost never see all of the behavior all of the time).

versions, and sets the last draft aside for a week to get a fresh perspective before he tackles the final report. However, his officemate, Hanna, may believe in group input, composing the report in group settings and showing the first draft to others for input before turning in a final version. A third performer, Lee, may wait for creative inspiration, then begin typing like crazy shortly before the report is due, perform a spell check, and turn in the resulting report.

All three reports may be outstanding, but they were produced in very different ways that reflect the individual differences of the report writers. If the manager happens to like Hanna's approach a little better than that of Luis or Lee, does that mean that the two of them should be forced to follow her behavior the next time they produce a report? Of course not. Each performer prepared versions of the report successfully, but because of different personalities, strengths, and preferences, each performer behaved differently and used different processes to prepare those reports. Focusing on behavior ignores individual differences, especially when flexibility may be more appropriate.

Basic Rule 20

Focusing on accomplishments or outcomes doesn't mean that how work is done is not important. If the process or method for achieving a result is critical, then that is part of the accomplishment. For instance, if the report not only needs to be accurate but also must include input from everyone on the team, then the accomplishment or outcome would be "producing an accurate report with full team input."

It's important to clarify a common misunderstanding about accomplishments. By focusing first on accomplishments or outcomes, some people confuse this principle with the argument that the end justifies the means. Stated another way, only the end product matters, not how it was accomplished. Nothing could be further from the truth when it comes to analyzing performance.

Recall that an accomplishment or outcome is what is of value to the organization. Outcomes expected of most managers are accurate and informed decisions. However, some managers may work with an office full of experienced, senior performers and it is critical that they be involved in management decisions. In this case, the accomplishment or outcome would be "accurate, informed decisions with staff participation." In other words, if *how* something is done is more critical than any result, it would be part of the accomplishment or performance outcome. Thus, accomplishments do not ignore or devalue process or behavior. To focus on accomplishments first is not saying that how something is done is irrelevant. If the process is a critical part of what the organization values, then the process becomes part of the performance outcome.

Here are some examples of where process is a key part of the accomplishment:

- ▸ a consensus decision (where buy-in is critical to how useful the decision is)
- ▸ completed report consistent with internal policy (where there is only one acceptable way to do things because of legal or ethical standards)
- ▸ ISO-compliant results (where work needs to follow ISO standards to ensure certification).

Think About This

A general rule is that to evaluate behavior it's usually necessary to observe it firsthand or talk to someone who did. But, accomplishments can be evaluated even if the performer is not around by verifying the accuracy of the report or counting the number of sales closed or seeing if customers are satisfied. If evaluation requires observation or presence, then it's probably behavior you're evaluating, not accomplishments.

It's important to be able to define what the specific accomplishment or outcome is that is expected from the performer. Whenever a client focuses on behavior, try to identify what outcome the behavior is supposed to produce. For instance, why is it critical for the analyst to work hard on the report? The result the client hopes to get from this hard work is a report that is thorough and delivered on time. Therefore, the necessary accomplishment, or outcome, is an accurate report on or before the deadline.

An accomplishment is usually something that can be measured even if the performer is absent or has gone home. To evaluate if someone hustles at work, it's necessary to watch that performer work; but to evaluate the performer's accomplishments, the evaluator can look at the completed work, count the sales totals, or read the report.

Clients frequently ask for solutions to change behavior. It is important to press the client on what results are expected from this behavior change. Often the behavior the client wants to focus on is irrelevant to the performance or may be caused by poor performance. In such cases, addressing the behavior solves nothing and certainly won't improve performance. A client may request conflict management training as a means of reducing staff bickering and in-fighting. When pressed, the client may insist that by reducing the conflict the staff will generate reports in a timely fashion. It may be that a bickering staff is annoying and visible, but it's probably not the reason reports are late. In fact, the staff may bicker because the reports aren't being done on time and people are casting blame at each other, in which case conflict management training will be a waste of time.

Noted

It is common for clients to request that consultants produce some kind of behavior change among a group of performers. The behavior could range from improving time management to taking more initiative to demonstrating leadership on the job. The first thing to do when faced with such requests is to determine what is supposed to happen if the behavior is changed. For instance, if the client asks for meeting management training because participants arrive late to meetings and are usually unprepared, push for the result that should occur if the behavior changes.

Think About This

Most clients won't be used to thinking in terms of accomplishments—they'll phrase things in terms of behavior. When they ask for improvement of a particular behavior (such as being friendly with customers) respond with "in order to do what" or "and this will change things in what way?" These questions should guide clients to provide the results or outcomes sought from the behavior change.

Initially, it's not easy to define accomplishments. But with just a little practice, identifying accomplishments can become second nature. Whenever a client specifies some behavior, the performance consultant should ask why the organization would pay someone to behave that way? That question should enable the consultant to identify some kind of accomplishment or outcome that explains what is really important to the organization. Remember, an accomplishment is what is of value to the organization. If the client wants to insist that some particular behavior is critical, try to find out if the work would be considered incomplete or insufficient without that behavior. If so, then it's a part of the accomplishment; and if not, then it's just a manager with stereotypes of how someone is supposed to look or behave.

It's important to distinguish between behavior that is truly part of the outcome or accomplishment versus behavior desired by the client. For instance, if a manager wants his or her staff to take more initiative at work, that's a desired behavior. While the manager may insist that the initiative is crucial to the performance, the real test of whether or not initiative is a part of the accomplishment is if the only result was initiative—would the organization be happy? But if the manager assumes that initiative will result in a faster work cycle, happier customers, and fewer mistakes (with less rework), then demonstrating initiative is not part of the accomplishment, it's a behavior or attribute that the manager believes will produce a particular outcome.

Think About This

To define an accomplishment, look at the requested behavior. What does the organization hope to get out of that behavior? For instance, if a client wants you to get staff to be friendlier to customers, it is hoped that this behavior will achieve customer satisfaction. If someone asks for more hustle, then respond with "and that will result in . . . ?" Often this will reveal the ulterior motive of the client and the source of the desired behavior improvement.

Basic Rule 21

It is usually more helpful to think about tasks rather than behavior. Tasks are the steps performers do to generate accomplishments.

How Behavior Still Figures Into the Equation

HPI starts by focusing on accomplishments or outcomes, not behavior. This does not mean that behavior is unimportant. But focusing first on behavior can cause misleading performance data. Behavior is critical in understanding performance, but accomplishments or outcomes come first in the analysis stage. Only after identification of outcomes is it possible to determine if there is a performance gap. The performance gap is in the accomplishment. Once it's clear there is a gap in accomplishment, then it makes sense to proceed to look at behavior.

It's usually not important to determine how people behave differently (which is what happens from focusing first on behavior). Focusing on outcomes, on the other hand, determines if there is a performance gap and identifies the best performers. Once this is done, it's possible to determine what behavior is critical (or irrelevant) to the accomplishment. From this point, the performance consultant will look at the tasks or behavior to understand how it contributes to performance (or the gap). Is the specific task something that other performers could learn to do, or is it a skill or ability that is uniquely rooted in this performer?

Think About This

Using the term *task* is preferable to that of behavior because task encourages the client to think about what is necessary to perform the job. Using the term *behavior* is distracting because it focuses on worker actions the client doesn't like but have no relevance to the level of performance. Focusing on the concept of tasks helps keep the focus on what matters.

Behavior is important to understanding performance—but only in the context of the accomplishments expected of the performer. Generally speaking, HPI refers to tasks rather than behavior. Once outcomes have been identified, it's important to determine the tasks that produce those accomplishments. In analyzing the critical tasks (usually by watching or interviewing performers), it's possible to identify some tasks that are irrelevant (or wasteful) to the result, some tasks that contribute to the accomplishment, and some tasks that are critical to producing what the organization wants.

Noted

It's very common for clients to say, "John is an excellent worker; he meets all of his goals. But, unless he stops behaving this particular way, I'm afraid I'll need to dismiss or reprimand him." What's wrong with that statement? How can John meet all of his expectations and be a great performer yet be someone the manager needs to dismiss? This constitutes a failure by the organization to clearly define the work outcomes. If there are certain behaviors that are critical to the job, then write them into the accomplishment. However, if those tasks are not critical to achieving the accomplishment, then the manager is guilty of arbitrarily assigning expectations for how a good performer looks and acts.

Identifying the Performance Gap

The purpose for being clear on all these concepts (accomplishments or outcomes and behaviors or tasks) is to identify performance gaps. Here is how that process of identifying performance gaps works. First, it's important to identify a key business goal or goals. Next, it's necessary to determine what performance (or outcome) drives that goal. The client may be able to answer that question or it may require the performance consultant to analyze what accomplishments are necessary to produce that result.

There will usually be several performance outcomes that are critical to achieving a particular business objective.

Noted

A performance gap is a difference between desired and actual accomplishments.

The next step is to determine what gaps exist with the performance. In other words, the performance consultant wants to find out if any of those accomplishments or outcomes isn't being met. Given that the client may have been focused on behaviors (or may not be clear what accomplishments are critical), this may be challenging. If the client has been measuring behavior (as demonstrated by a series of performance appraisals or supervisor reports indicating that Ramon talks too long on the phone, Julia is too informal with clients, and Horst talks too much in meetings), then it may not be initially clear if there is a performance gap. Until there is clarity that there is a performance gap, the performance consultant shouldn't be interested in a behavior gap.

Basic Rule 22

Performance gaps involve accomplishments or outcomes (so it's possible to measure the degree of the gap), not behavior.

Think About This

If a client phrases a performance gap in terms of behavior ("Jeff needs to explain more product details to the client"), ask the client to express this in terms of accomplishments or outcomes. Behavior is misleading. If Jeff has similar results when compared with other customer reps, then his lack of explanation of product detail may not be an issue. Don't let the client phrase a performance gap in terms of behavior.

Once the right accomplishments have been identified, it's valuable to compare ideal versus actual performance. In other words, what is the target accomplishment, where are the performers in actuality, and how much difference is there between these two levels? This is what produces the performance gap—the difference between desired and actual accomplishment levels. Because the focus is on accomplishments rather than behavior, the performance gap is usually explained in a quantitative measure or number.

Here is an example to better understand the process of identifying performance gaps. The manager of a customer call center has a performance problem. The primary business goal is to achieve an 83 percent rating on their customer satisfaction index (CSI) for the next quarter. Currently, the call center is achieving a 59 percent rating, falling very short of the goal.

Basic Rule 23

Phrase the performance gap so that's it's quantitative. For instance: Calls answered within two rings instead of the current five rings (a gap of three rings), or number of reports completed on time instead of an average of two days late.

The manager claims that there are three key performance drivers to achieve a high CSI score. First, all calls need to be answered within two rings or less. Second, callers must perceive the customer service representative as knowledgeable and credible with their service problem. When pressed, the manager indicates that there are follow-up calls and focus groups made to representative groups of customers to track perceived credibility of center reps. Using a scale, the target for credibility is a 4.0 or higher on a scale of five. Third, results have shown that callers who are transferred within the center or placed on hold (to talk to a manager) are significantly less satisfied than those who have problems resolved by the center rep who originally answers the phone.

Once the critical performance drivers have been identified, it is important to determine if there are performance gaps with any of those drivers. If there aren't any (yet the business goal isn't being met), then that means that there must be other accomplishments that are more important than those identified as the key performance drivers. Further inquiry demonstrates that there are performance gaps in the three key drivers for the business goal.

Instead of answering all calls within two rings, the average number of rings is 3.2 (which means that since some calls are answered in one or two rings, many others aren't answered until four or five rings). The credibility rating (that customers have of the call reps) is 4.3 on a scale of 5.0, so the perceived expertise and trustworthiness of the center reps seems fine.

Finally, tracking data within the center shows that only 82 percent (instead of the desired 95 percent) of all calls are resolved without transferring the caller or putting him or her on hold. Thus, there are two performance gaps that appear to be significant (a gap of 1.2 rings and a gap of 13 percent in transfer/hold). The next step would be to determine what tasks are involved in answering the calls quickly without placing customers on hold or transferring them. In identifying these tasks, it's important to distinguish between irrelevant behavior (for instance, just because the call center rep with the best transfer/hold rate also doodles on scrap paper doesn't mean all other reps should be required to doodle

Think About This

There will oftentimes be more than one performance gap responsible for the failure to meet a business goal. That is why it's important to sort out what performance is critical for a particular goal.

while they work) and critical tasks (the best call center rep may also have all of her reference materials up-to-date and within reach so she rarely has to put people on hold to seek answers).

Basic Rule 24

Exemplars or top performers are employees who do an outstanding job at particular accomplishments. By analyzing how these exemplars achieve their results, it's possible to find short cuts to improve performance across the organization.

Spotting the Exemplar

One of the best ways to improve performance is through leveraging information gained through outstanding employees. Once an outstanding performer is identified, that employee can then be used to understand how to improve performance for all of the staff. These performers are sometimes referred to as exemplars. Exemplars can provide examples of just how much performance can be improved and may represent realistic ceilings for performance goals. However, exemplars are even more useful in figuring out how to improve performance. By looking at what exemplary performers do that make them exemplary, it's possible to identify what tasks are critical to boosting performance as well as new ways of doing things that might get better results.

How do performance consultants identify exemplary performers? Sometimes this is challenging. Because many organizations tend to focus on behavior, people who've been identified as star employees by management may actually be mediocre in terms of their performance accomplishments. Often, management's star employee is a worker who just fits the pictures managers have of how people are supposed to behave. Using such a performer as an exemplar is not only a waste of time but counterproductive. A performance consultant could analyze

Noted

Exemplars are one of the quickest ways to boost performance because, instead of theories or ideas from other organizations about improving performance, the exemplars have proven what can generate better results in their organization.

such a performer and end up adopting approaches that actually decrease overall performance. Remember, the objective is not to get everyone to behave the same way; it's to determine how to get good results. It doesn't matter if three people write reports differently as long as the final products meet the performance standards. This just highlights the importance of focusing on accomplishments so performance is measured objectively, rather than emphasizing competencies or behavior.

Management often can't identify who the top performers are, and, in addition, the top performers often can't explain why they outperform everyone else. The lack of measurement results in a kind of ignorance about exemplary performance that is common in many organizations.

There may be times where the true exemplar in an office or team is regarded as a bit of an odd duck. This is because many exemplars prefer to do things their own way, may have developed new processes or tools, or often have a focus for the work that is different from other performers. Thus, they may not appear to fit in with the rest of the team. Also, there may be no one overall exemplary performer. Instead, it may be a case of several employees—none of whom is outstanding across the board—who outperform everyone else in one particular category (so the exemplary performance is in individual elements of work).

Within a salesforce there may be an exemplar at closing sales, another at researching clients, and another at preparing proposals. Each of three performers may have significantly better accomplishments than their peers in their area of expertise, but be average at other areas. The purpose here is not to put someone on a pedestal. Instead, it's to find a performer who has already discovered some of the secrets of how to get better performance in at least one area.

Think About This

Don't take management's word for who is or is not an exemplar. Always confirm who the exemplar is with data about performer results. The findings are often surprising to management.

Think About This

Exemplars don't need to be role models. They are performers who have found a way to achieve better accomplishments than their peers.

According to Jim Fuller and Jeanne Farrington (1999), among the things that differentiate top performers from their peers are that exemplars:

▶ do away with unnecessary steps
▶ perform an extra step that is needed but not documented
▶ use available information and documentation that others do not
▶ utilize a self-created job aid that others do not
▶ employ information or data that others do not
▶ possess better tools than others
▶ have a different motive for performing
▶ receive different guidance and feedback
▶ obtain different incentives.

Think About This

Often it isn't cost effective to eliminate a performance gap. In this situation, the performance consultant needs to manage client expectations.

It's also important to manage client expectations around performance gaps. The client may expect the performance consultant to solve or eliminate the performance issue. In reality, there are usually many causes to any performance gap (and many performance gaps that contribute to the failure to achieve a key business goal). The solutions required to close, perhaps 80 percent of a gap, may be realistic and affordable. But, the amount of work and expense to totally eliminate the gap may actually have a negative return-on-investment. Part of what the performance consultant brings to the table for the client is objectivity.

Getting It Done

Identifying the performance gap is at the heart of what performance consultants do. Yet too many managers and clients fail to effectively analyze what the key performance is, discern what kind of gap exists, and figure out how to measure the gap. By applying the concepts from this chapter, you'll be able to see how clients go wrong in attempts to assess performance issues.

Exercise 4-1 identifies some activities to help you apply some of the key points from this chapter and improve your performance consulting expertise.

Exercise 4-1. Focusing on accomplishments.

1. Identify what accomplishments you're accountable for. Start with your résumé and convert the behaviors, skills, and knowledge to accomplishments. Then move to your most recent performance appraisal or the most recent set of performance objectives you've been given. Convert them to accomplishments that are time bound and measurable.

2. At work or with a recent client, review the business goals for an office or department. Which goals appear to be ones that are measurable and time bound? If they aren't measurable or time bound, how could they be converted so they would be? What performance appears to drive those goals? And, what goals does the organization espouse that appear to be goals but actually are not? (An example would be a "goal" of improving morale because the organization wants to decrease turnover.)

3. Identify at least one example of a situation in which an intervention was selected to deal with a specific behavior (such as time management to improve how fast people work, or conflict management to stop bickering and disagreement) and then the organization rationalized that this change in behavior would lead to significant business value (such as increased productivity or improved customer service or shortened cycle time). Then, start with the business goal used to rationalize this intervention and work backward by identifying key performance drivers and what performance gaps exist among these drivers.

(continued on page 68)

Exercise 4-1. Focusing on accomplishments (continued).

4. Look at whom management identifies as a star employee. What measurable accomplishments does this performer show, or is he or she they viewed as a top employee because of behavior? If you were to identify an exemplar in your organization, what accomplishments would you use to distinguish between the exemplar and the other performers?

Performance gaps help you hone in on what is going wrong and how to measure it. Until you know why the gap exists you don't know what will fix it. This is where the root cause analysis comes in: By identifying the root cause to the performance gap, you'll be able to determine the correct solution. The next chapter looks at root cause analysis.

5

Performance Consulting Finds the Root Cause

What's Inside This Chapter

Here you'll find out:

▶ Why root cause analysis is so critical for effective performance consulting work

▶ How to do a root cause analysis and some tools to help you do it

▶ Categories of root causes for performance gaps

▶ Common mistakes that consultants make in identifying the root cause of performance gaps.

Flavor of the Month

Think of all of the fads, temporary fixes, Band-Aid approaches, and latest crazes that occur in organizations. Organizations are quick to place their hope on fads in an effort to find a quick fix to problems. The result tends to be time and energy wasted on actions that don't solve problems. All these situations represent missed opportunities to do something good.

Plenty of experienced professionals have grown cynical with efforts to improve performance or change things because of all of the false steps and mistaken ideas they've seen in their careers. In short, most organizations are guilty of a series of wrong-headed efforts to implement answers that won't solve the problems they were intended to address (Argyris, 1986). The primary reason for this is that most decision makers fail to get to the true cause of the particular performance gap. This isn't for lack of trying or interest in solving the problem, but most performers grappling with performance issues are guilty of not bringing a rigorous and objective perspective to understanding the gap. Consequently, there is usually no effort to get to the cause of the problem, or, if there is, it is superficial and inadequate.

Noted

As a graduate student, I took a course that had a combination of students from different degree programs, including sociology, communication, public administration, and business. Assigned to study groups by area of discipline, each team brought unique perspectives on an assigned case study. The sociology graduate students thought the answer involved changing the organizational culture of the company. The public administration students believed that the organization in the case study needed more explicit policies and procedures. The communication representatives argued that the answer involved better information processes internally, and the business students believed management didn't have enough power to fire poor performers. In short, every group's superficial answer was determined by the members' individual perspectives and was not informed by an in-depth analysis of what was really causing issues within the case study.

As a consequence of how most organizations approach performance issues, interventions are picked on the basis of biased perspective, limiting the true understanding of the cause of the problem. Until the true cause of a performance gap is identified, it isn't possible to close the gap except by accident.

The Critical Importance of Root Cause Analysis

The process of determining the root cause of a performance gap is one of the distinguishing elements between performance consulting and other approaches to dealing with issues at work.

Basic Rule 25

The best way to avoid perceptual bias about performance issues is:
1) do a root cause analysis and 2) be systematic in the analysis. Don't jump to conclusions about the nature of the performance problem or its solution.

Basic Rule 26

Identifying the root cause of the performance gap makes determining a solution easy because the root cause dictates the appropriate solution. Without knowing the true root cause, it's just a guessing game as to what solution will work.

Too many other approaches fail to figure what is really causing the problem; rather, they rush to the solution stage and end up being a waste of time and resources. Alternatively, decision makers may be so convinced that they know what the problem is all about that they don't see a need to go through a rigorous process. They think they know why performance isn't happening.

But, performance consultants can't operate on instinct—it's necessary to confirm with data. Performance consultants don't jump to conclusions; they withhold judgment until after a rigorous analysis. Good performance consultants do use instinct and experience in their analysis, but they don't let these attributes bias their assessment of why performance gaps exist.

Why Organizations Fail at Analyzing Causes

Most efforts at solving performance problems fail because they involve the wrong solution. Why do so many organizations end up with the wrong solution?

> ▶ Too many organizations, consultants, and clients are in a hurry and rush the analysis process. Analyzing performance problems and gathering the necessary data does not need to take a long time. But, so many organizations face such tremendous time pressure that performance consultants hear from clients the equivalent of the Queen of Hearts' line from *Alice in Wonderland:* "Sentence first, verdict afterwards!" The client's position basically is that

Noted

Many HRD professionals believe they've done some form of cause analysis when they actually have not. Typically, clients request solutions such as training without having identified the real cause of the performance gap. A basic needs analysis almost always can show that communication skills within all organizations are lacking. Is this a good cause analysis? No. It didn't start with the business goal and identification of a performance gap. There are many reasons why people might have poor communication skills, yet without knowing the performance gap and root cause, it isn't possible to determine if communication skills are a major factor in the failure to get the business results. Stated differently, just because performers are weak at a particular skill (such as communication) doesn't mean that skill deficiency is critical to the performance gap. It's not enough to find an area that people are weak in; a good performance consultant identifies whether that deficiency is critical to the performance necessary to meeting the business objective.

"There's no time to spend time figuring out the cause of the problem—just do something!" This urgency leads to mistakes and interventions that solve nothing. Ironically, front-end analysis doesn't have to involve a large time commitment; in many cases, a proper root cause analysis leads to solutions that not only work, but also take less time to implement than the Band-Aid solutions originally requested by the client.

▶ Too many clients and consultants are convinced they already know the answer without having to look at the data. This tendency leads to premature decisions based on anecdotal evidence. Research in leadership is replete with

Think About This

If clients are convinced they already know the cause, arguing with them almost never works. Instead of arguing for the need to do a root cause analysis, tell the client you need a little time to get acclimated to the workforce and the organization's culture. Don't call it a root cause analysis or a front-end analysis, but do use this time to gather data and marshal facts.

examples where decision makers were positive they didn't need data because they thought they already knew the answer (Argyris, 1993).

▶ Clients sometimes confuse symptoms with the cause (Mager & Pipe, 1997). For instance, a team with poor performance may blame it on high turnover if many team members are leaving. But, analysis of the problem may show that the gap predates any turnover, thus proving that retention is not the cause of the performance issue. Organizations (such as this team) that do poorly tend to have higher turnover because people don't want to be associated with a failure. There are plenty of other examples of how a superficial analysis confuses symptoms with causes; merely addressing the symptoms won't solve the performance problem.

Think About This

Remember—clients tend to focus mostly on behavior. Clients like to go for what is most visible. Whenever a client says that the cause is a specific behavior ("Giuseppe doesn't listen" or "Karen talks too much"), it's critical to pull the conversation back to accomplishments.

▶ No one is intentionally biased toward a particular decision. But, as Chris Argyris (1986) has shown with his work on mental models, people's perspective limits their ability to "see" issues; they truly become blind to things. Trainers tend to see every problem as a training problem (knowledge and skills deficiency). Experience often makes it easy to rationalize not doing a

Think About This

When a client appears locked into a particular explanation as the cause of a performance gap, arguing against that cause is usually a waste of time. The performance consultant is probably better off getting the client to admit that there may be other factors at work. It's easier for a client to agree that there are multiple possible causes rather than to admit that the initial explanation of the cause was wrong.

root cause analysis. This is an especially big problem for clients because their background and expertise shape what they perceive and the menu of answers that they think is available to them.

▶ Too often, new performance consultants stop at the first plausible cause they come to and fail to identify *all* causes behind a performance gap. It's vital to identify them to determine which causes have the most impact on the performance issue at hand. A variation on this theme may involve identifying a range of causes but not probing deep enough to find the root cause of the problem.

Think About This

Oftentimes what happens when a client is guilty of perceptual bias (being committed to a particular viewpoint and blind to other perspectives), it's a case of acting on anecdotal evidence. The client probably has one or two obvious examples to support a sweeping generalization of the problem cause.

Some performance consultants look at causes for performance gaps but don't go far enough. These consultants are guilty of failing to get to the root cause, of stopping the cause analysis process too soon. Here is one example to illustrate this failure: The performer in this case is the administrative assistant for the regional manager of operations. The administrative assistant is expected to have completed the status reports for the regional manager by Friday noon every week. But, the reports are going out by the close of business or later on Fridays, which means management doesn't get them until Monday sometimes and also leads to overtime pay for the administrative assistant. The performance gap indicates that it takes an average of five hours to prepare such reports for other administrative assistants in other regions, but it takes an average of 10 hours for the assistant in this region. What is the cause of this performance gap?

A performance consultant examines performers in similar roles and finds that other administrative assistants can collate the information in approximately 90 minutes, although the performer in question averages four hours. It sounds like the root cause is probably a skill deficiency (the ability to collate report data)—right? Training on how to collate data (such as a technical writing course) sounds like it would be just the ticket. Not so fast.

Why does this particular administrative assistant take so long to collate this data? The performance consultant looks at data from other performers and discovers that other regions send data to the administrative assistants in electronic format with standard templates. But, the performer in question gets information from a range of documents, including some numbers scrawled on restaurant napkins, with a mixture of formats and measures. So, the cause of the "taking longer time to collate data" performance gap is that operations personnel don't use a standard format for information that is required for submission to the administrative assistant.

It sounds as if the problem can be solved by sending operations personnel to a special class on submitting data. The problem with this assumption is that there is no proof the performers (operations personnel) lack the skills or knowledge on how to submit the data. The performance consultant may even discover that these personnel are able and willing to submit data using an electronic template but their regional manager doesn't require that they do so.

Therefore, the root cause in this case is the failure of the regional manager to require staff to use a standard format for submitting weekly data to the administrative assistant. In short, the reason why the regional manager isn't getting her reports on time is because of her policy (or lack of one) on how staff should submit data to the administrative assistant. Sending the administrative assistant to training will fail. Training the operations staff will fail. But, having the manager establish a policy and then enforcing that policy on submitting data for the weekly report in a standard format has a chance of succeeding because *it addresses the root cause of the problem.*

Basic Rule 27

A root cause analysis doesn't have to take a lot of time or a great deal of effort. But, an effective root cause analysis does require good data and objectivity.

There is also a tendency to look at where the problem first appears and then appoint that location the source or cause of the problem. Oftentimes, the problem appears in one location (loading dock fills incorrect orders), but the cause is further back in the process (the salesforce takes orders by hand, but the handwriting is difficult to read, leading to incorrect shipping by the dock crew).

Causes of Performance Gaps

There are potentially thousands of root causes for performance gaps, but for clarity's sake it makes sense to categorize these root causes. Ethan Sanders and Sivasailam Thiagarajan (2002) developed a particularly effective model for ASTD. According to these two collaborators, root causes break down into six boxes or categories:

- ▶ structure/process
- ▶ resources
- ▶ information
- ▶ knowledge/skills
- ▶ motives
- ▶ wellness.

Structure/Process

This root cause category has to do with how the organization is set up and the processes that are relevant to the work. The larger organizations become, the more likely they are to have process issues (Rummler & Brache, 1990). Organizational policies, workflow, mission, and the business's organization all fall into this category. Support processes such as performance appraisal, hiring, and benefits administration are also examples of processes that can covertly create problems with production.

Resources

This tends to be a cop-out answer for many performers and clients. This response often is phrased by clients as "If we only had more staff/more time/a bigger budget, then we'd be able to solve the problem." Of course, such is rarely the case, but the

Think About This

To the extent clients attribute structure/process as a "root cause," they usually phrase it as a solution ("If we only eliminated these rules, I'd be able to produce more widgets" or "If I didn't have to wait on Ted and Maria to input the data, I'd be able to finish the report on time"). If it is phrased as a solution, don't accept it as a legitimate root cause; dig deeper and get more data to determine what the real cause is.

root cause of a performance problem may be a bottleneck caused by insufficient resources at a particular part of the workflow. Resources could include such things as adequate office space, appropriate computer power, the right tools, staffing, budget, time, or even political clout.

Think About This

Oftentimes, a resource root cause involves the quality of a tool. For example, the performer doesn't have the right tool for the job or has inadequate equipment. In other cases, the organization has sufficient resources within an office or department but has allocated them poorly. For example, too many people are taking calls, and not enough are available to answer correspondence. Don't let clients argue that if only they had more staff or money they'd be able to solve the problem. This approach ignores how the current performance or processes may be contributing to the problem. Throwing money at performance issues rarely solves them and often makes them worse.

Information

Joe Harless (1996) observes that the lack of timely and accurate feedback is the most common root cause for performance problems he has encountered in his practice. Many and varied causes of performance gaps exist, but knowledge and skills are not among the top causes (Csoka, 1994). As work becomes more complex and performers specialize or have narrower roles, coordination becomes critical. Coordination requires information about who is doing what, work schedules, changes in plans, new roles, customer input, feedback to adjust performance, and clear expectations or standards for work.

Think About This

Sometimes the issue isn't what information is shared but how or when it's communicated. For instance, messages that are given in stressful situations are more likely to be missed, and feedback that occurs substantially after the performance is less likely to change behavior.

Knowledge/Skills

Trainers know all about this root cause. Under this category, performers either don't know how or aren't able to perform the work. However, this is usually more than just a case of lacking knowledge or skills. The performers may have skills confused (they have the right skills but apply them incorrectly or in the wrong sequence). Alternatively, performers may have the knowledge, but they aren't able to recall it when necessary, or they may use the knowledge infrequently so there is a problem with remembering the proper performance.

Think About This

It is easy to misdiagnose knowledge and skills root causes. Whenever performers appear unable to do particular work, the gap appears to be a "training problem." Try this quick test to see if the root cause deals with knowledge and skills: If performers were offered a huge bonus for doing the work correctly, could they perform up to standard? If so, then it's not about knowledge and skills but due to some other cause. Another test for knowledge and skills is to see if the performers were ever able to do the performance correctly. If so, then the subsequent performance gap is not likely to be caused by a knowledge/skills issue unless performers have forgotten the skill.

Motives

Clients blame motives all the time ("Katia is unmotivated; that's why she does such poor work!"). The motives category is actually much more subtle and complex. Motives are not like a light switch; it's not true that either people are motivated and "on" or unmotivated and "off." Workers are always motivated, but the motives may not be the same as the manager's. This discrepancy can lead to a variety of root causes for performance gaps. There may be misguided rewards (such as workers are encouraged to work slowly because when they work faster they are given more work). Access to information, compensation, trust, respect, peer pressure—all of these can lead to issues that determine what performers are motivated to do and how hard they're encouraged to work.

Think About This

A quick test for motives root causes is to find out what kinds of behavior and results are rewarded. The organization may have official responses ("Hard work is rewarded here"), but then there is the reality ("When I work hard I don't get to go home early, so instead I just try to look busy").

Wellness

This broad category includes a host of issues, ranging from physical health to emotional stability to substance abuse to alertness. Long shifts or late-night work can lead to reduced concentration because of fatigue. Problems at home can reduce concentration. Physical or emotional disorders can take people away from work or reduce their productivity while they are at work.

Think About This

Many wellness issues are hidden and difficult to discover because of employee assistance program policies, nondisclosure rules with HR, or a range of policies established to reduce discrimination. Consequently, the best way to identify these root causes depends upon the performance consultant's ability to build trust so that workers are comfortable disclosing what they see.

How to Do a Root Cause Analysis

Doing a root cause analysis is pretty easy, but it requires objectivity to avoid jumping to conclusions and guarding against bias. It involves a willingness to explore (so very rigid or dogmatic people may have trouble doing this work). And, it requires a systematic approach to the analysis (so key evidence isn't ignored). Performers with strong quality or Six Sigma backgrounds have valuable expertise at root cause analysis and are ideal resources for analysis work.

Basic Rule 28

Human error isn't a root cause—there is always a preceding cause to any human mistake.

It isn't sufficient to indicate as a root cause that someone made a mistake ("Hui-Hsing put on the wrong part" or "Abdul reversed the numbers on the form" or "Colin gave incorrect information to the customer"). The root cause analysis focus should not be on whom to blame but why the problem happened and how to prevent it from happening again. If the package was sent to the wrong address because the agent wrote down the wrong address on the package, it's important to know why this happened so the solution can correct it. If it isn't clear why the performer made the error, then it won't be clear what action will solve the problem and prevent the error from happening again.

Basic Rule 29

Most performance gaps have multiple causes. It may not be possible to address all of them.

It may be helpful to examine a case of root case analysis in action. Imagine a manager named Dieter. One of Dieter's accomplishments is "an informed office with up-to-date information." However, Dieter's staff is rarely informed about what is going on, and they hear key information only very late in the process rather than in a timely fashion. It appears that there is a gap between what Dieter's staff is supposed to be informed about and what information they actually get from Dieter.

The initial causes for this gap are the following: Dieter fails to give timely feedback to help correct mistakes by staff, and Dieter never schedules staff meetings to share information. Absent any further analysis, it isn't clear why Dieter fails to provide feedback and hold staff meetings. Maybe he doesn't know how to provide feedback or how to plan and conduct a meeting (which involves skills and, therefore, training is the answer). Perhaps he thinks staff already knows this information (which involves incorrect information on his part and, therefore, coaching or employee feedback is the answer). Maybe he likes keeping his staff uninformed and views the control of information as crucial to maintaining power (which involves motivation and, therefore, has implications for motivational solutions).

It's necessary to push the cause analysis at least one level further to identify the root cause—because human error (Dieter fails to communicate with his staff) can't be a root cause. In this case, further exploration demonstrates that Dieter is so over-burdened with meetings and priorities from senior management that he has little time for his staff. Thus, the root cause falls into the category of resources: Dieter is rarely in the office. When he is there, he's usually responding to calls from other managers or his senior manager, so he has no time to supervise his own staff, provide feedback, or hold staff meetings to share information.

Think About This

Imagine a hypothetical work process consisting of 15 steps from start to completion. Problems may appear at step 12 but actually be caused in step 9 of the work process. Even when it appears the root cause has been identified and where it originates, it's important to test the analysis by seeing if there is an explanation for how the problem could originate earlier in a work process.

How far should a root cause analysis go? The performance consultant must use common sense. It makes no sense to push a root cause analysis to causal levels that extend outside of the organization, such as the state of the economy or human nature. Additionally, remember the purpose for conducting the root cause analysis in the first place: to identify an intervention to solve the problem. This is not science seeking to establish a causal relationship. Therefore, the performance consultant should push the root cause analysis as far as it seems useful and applicable.

A hypothetical example can illustrate how the root cause analysis works. Imagine that at a certain organization, it is found that 20 percent of the building's doors are left unlocked and unchecked after hours. It is clear that there is a performance gap with the security guards.

The root cause analysis establishes that the doors are left unlocked and unchecked because the guards on the late shift think those doors have already been checked or the guards lose track of which doors have been locked. Why does this happen? The guards are sleepy and, therefore, have poor short-term memory and comprehension. Why are they sleepy? Many of the guards work multiple shifts doing security at this organization and then another shift for another company. Why do many work multiple shifts? They need the money because their jobs pay so poorly. Why is their economic status such that one job won't provide sufficient income? At this point the root cause analysis has gone too far. What's of value for the performance consultant is to know this: The guards are sleepy and are likely to remain sleepy unless the company can find a way to get people who only work one shift. The solution is likely to involve either paying the guards more (so they don't work two jobs) or recruiting security personnel who would only seek to work one shift and probably get enough sleep.

Once a performance gap has been identified, it's important to determine why the gap persists. This is the process of a root cause analysis. Although there are a

Basic Rule 30

Don't push the root cause analysis beyond the boundaries of the organization. If the root cause identified involves large societal forces or human nature, then it is a line of analysis that is not workable as a tool for closing performance gaps.

Noted

It's not enough to find one example of a breakdown and what caused it. It's necessary to understand why the problem persists. The front-end analysis may discover that the reason why packages are mailed with incorrect addresses is because of sloppy recordkeeping by the shipping department, but the reason why the sloppiness persists is because the manager thinks that the records aren't necessary. Until this situation is solved (the manager's motivation to encourage accurate records), there won't be an improvement in the recordkeeping by the shipping clerks.

variety of different techniques that individual performance consultants use to conduct root cause analysis, the techniques primarily boil down to gathering information, testing theories, and being systematic in the analysis.

What tools are available for identifying the root cause of a performance gap? The quality field has developed a wide range of tools for doing a root cause analysis. One of the more common root cause tools comes out of Toyota (Ohno, 1995) and is referred to as the "Five Why's" or a "Why Tree." In this approach, performance consultants ask "why" repeatedly until they believe they have gotten to the appropriate level of analysis. Because there are multiple causes to most performance gaps, charting the answers produces a graphic that looks somewhat like a tree with branches of words (figure 5-1).

It's not critical to use the word "why" for the Why Tree to be successful. For instance, a consultant could ask "How did that happen?" or "What was the explanation for that?" or "What preceded that?" or "What precipitated that?" The key point is that the performance consultant views the performance gap as an onion, and it's time to peel back layer after layer until you get to the center and find the root cause in the core.

Noted

Another approach for analyzing the root cause is Kepner and Tregoe's 1965 model for Is/Is Not boundary setting. This model can help identify where the problem originates by also defining where the problem doesn't reside. There are also process maps and flowcharting approaches and tools that can depict a range of activities including the major steps of a process, what happens at each stage of a process, the movement of people, and who is responsible for particular actions.

Another tool for doing a root cause analysis is the Ishikawa or fishbone diagram (Ishikawa, 1969). The Ishikawa diagram (figure 5-2) is a drawing of a fish spine with bones leading from the spine. Each bone represents a major cause area such as resources, process, skills, and so on. As potential causes are identified, they are drawn off of the major bones to show connection to cause areas. The Ishikawa diagram is an excellent tool to discourage performance consultants from letting their experience as a trainer or OD consultant bias their perspective.

Figure 5-1. An example of a Why Tree.

Let's suppose you're trying to understand why managers don't complete performance appraisals by stated deadlines. Using the Why Tree tool, you generate the following results:

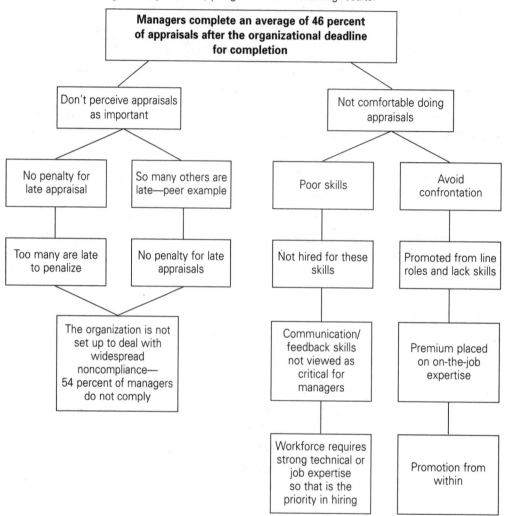

As you can see, not all branches of this Why Tree extend five levels because you either couldn't go any further or because it made no sense to proceed further. However, given three root causes (The organization isn't set up to deal with 54 percent of managers in noncompliance so no action is taken; managers come from the line and are promoted from within; and workforce requires strong technical expertise so that is the priority in hiring), three types of solutions are available to you. First, change the system so managers who don't submit appraisals face some kind of penalty. Second, make communications skills a higher priority when hiring personnel. Third, either hire managers with those skills (thus, not promoting from within) or provide those appraisal skills for managers promoted from the ranks.

Figure 5-2. An example of an Ishikawa diagram.

Why does the engineering department fail to meet project milestones in time?

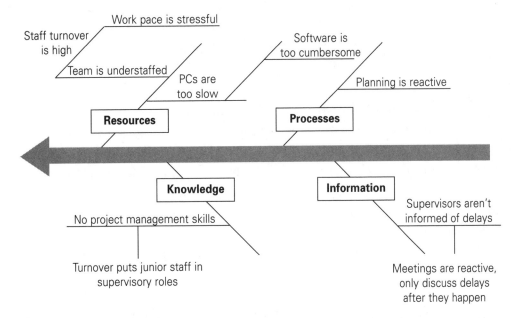

By looking at this simple version of an Ishikawa diagram, you can see that for a variety of reasons, inexperienced staff end up in supervisory roles and that meetings to coordinate project work aren't proactive (upcoming work is not discussed, only milestones that have already been missed). The solution to the problem of the engineering department falling behind on project deadlines is through a combination of improving skills (either training junior staff or keeping senior staff with project management skills) and restructuring planning meetings (through training, job aids, or the use of facilitators).

Think About This

The Ishikawa diagram fits nicely with the Sanders/Thiagarajan six-box model for categories of root causes. Just draw six major bones off the spine and label them Structure/Process, Resources, Information, Knowledge/Skills, Motives, and Wellness.

Basic Rule 31

Good performance consultants tap into other resources within the organization. Six Sigma or quality professionals have strong backgrounds in root cause analysis and a range of useful tools as well. Look to partner with these professionals when doing front-end analysis work.

Getting It Done

The root cause analysis element of the HPI process is critical. This is typically the element of the process that is least accessible to most executives and clients. If you master this element of the process, selecting the correct solution becomes much easier. Getting the root cause analysis down is the difference between a solution that works versus a Band-Aid approach that's a temporary fix at best.

Exercise 5-1 offers some opportunities for you to apply what has been covered in this chapter.

Exercise 5-1. Thinking about root cause analysis.

1. Identify possible resources in your organization (or among your clients) that have some expertise with root cause analysis. If there isn't a formal quality or Six Sigma department within your organization, look for performers who have experience in these areas. Once you've identified potential resources, think about how you can pull them into potential projects and take advantage of their expertise.

2. Besides the tools identified in this book, there are a range of different techniques for doing root cause analysis. Identify at least two different tools, and practice with them so that you have a high comfort level using either tool. You might start by looking at a recent training request (even if it's one you've already provided the training for) and do a root cause analysis to see what the real problem is. Don't forget to look beyond knowledge and skills causes.

3. Review the section of this chapter that discusses the ways in which organizations make mistakes with root cause analysis. Which ones do you see most frequently with your clients? Once you've identified the most frequent mistakes in cause analysis, develop strategies for dealing with those failed approaches.

4. Are there root cause areas (such as knowledge and skills) that your organization tends to focus on disproportionately? Are there other root causes (such as process or information) that are almost completely ignored? If so, this is useful information about your organization's culture as well as potential blind spots that clients and managers may have.

In the next chapter, you'll look at data collection methods and processes. This information is helpful for all stages of the front-end analysis and for evaluation work.

6
Performance Consulting Does Not Jump to Conclusions

▪▪

What's Inside This Chapter

Here you'll see how to:

▶ Be rigorous and systematic in your analysis
▶ Employ methods for being quick yet thorough
▶ Use data collection and analysis effectively
▶ Discuss performance issues with clients in various situations.

HPI and Other Approaches

Performance consultants use various approaches to deal with performance issues at work. Although there are a number of procedural differences between performance consulting and other schools, the biggest overall difference between how performance consultants approach issues versus the way clients and managers typically approach them is the degree of rigor that HPI demands. In short, performance consultants don't jump to conclusions but work to overcome the biases that are natural in any analysis. Performance consultants are systematic in their approach, and, thus, the result is more likely to be objective and accurate.

Noted

Individuals who are convinced they are objective can be quite guilty of biased perception (Argyris, 1986). This is not a factor of experience or intelligence. Chris Argyris argues that part of the distinction between what he calls type I learning, which is circular and reinforces biases, and type II learning, which is more objective and examines assumptions, is that type II learning looks at assumptions, is systematic, avoids jumping to conclusions, tests conclusions, and considers a range of data. HPI, then, is consistent with the type II learning approach.

Basic Rule 32

Performance consulting demands objectivity. Bias is inherent in any analysis, so it's critical to use methods and approaches that compensate for bias.

Subjectivity and Performance

Clients are almost always positive that they know what the problem is as well as its root cause. Furthermore, clients are almost always certain that they know more about the problem than any consultant does. To accuse clients of not being objective is fatuous; it doesn't work. The fact that it doesn't work does not mean that clients are objective. Clients—for a wide range of reasons—are not likely to be objective about their problems. They usually jump to conclusions, form premature analysis, act without a root cause analysis, and assume something is critical without confirming business goals. As performance consultants, a systematic and objective approach to problems is a big part of the value that the HPI process brings to clients.

Basic Rule 33

To conduct an objective analysis, it's essential to admit to existing biases, follow a process to prevent premature conclusions, and attempt to base conclusions on data and measures.

Practically every performance improvement project involves a learning curve. This is especially true if it's a first-time client or if it's a reactive situation in which the project was initiated by the client rather than the performance consultant. This explains why, at least in part, the client feels comfortable dictating solutions. Additionally, the typical approach in the past is that when clients called up trainers, clients told the trainers what they wanted, and then trainers provided it. This transactional approach does not work in performance consulting. Also, clients tend to assume that they're the experts and, therefore, the most knowledgeable people when it comes to the performance gaps within their organization.

Noted

Clients assume they know more because usually they have more exposure to the work setting than the consultants. They assume this gives them greater insight into the problem. In reality, although clients may have some background knowledge, it also leads to some shortsightedness on their part. The client's knowledge isn't deeper than the performance consultant's; it's just different knowledge (company background and product knowledge versus an understanding of performance). Finally, trainers and HRD professionals generally aren't very credible when it comes to operational issues or finance and business results, further complicating discussions between clients and performance consultants.

Basic Rule 34
Never treat clients' statements as factual. Sometimes clients' perceptions are accurate, but their perceptions are usually colored by biases. Start with their opinion, but check and verify what they say.

Traditionally, trainers take clients at their word. If clients ask for specific training classes, trainers tend to believe the request is necessary. Trainers then usually do a needs assessment to determine what that workshop should look like and what competencies it should cover. Trainers almost never go into such a request seeking to prove that the request is unfounded or what other factors might be more important than training. When trainers decide which courses to offer for the next fiscal year, they typically survey managers in the organization and ask what training should be offered or what their employees need. In short, trainers are often guilty of relying on the client's diagnosis of the situation.

On the other hand, performance consultants need to be skeptical of what clients say. Performance consultants need good critical thinking and listening ability (to decipher client comments and recognize the difference between fact and speculation). Performance consultants also need to be very diplomatic so they can adroitly explain why time invested in front-end analysis work makes sense when the clients are convinced they know what the intervention should be.

Noted

Good performance consultants are effective at balancing the competing demands of treating clients with respect and honoring their responses while remaining skeptical and questioning of everything the clients say.

As a performance consultant, there is (at least) a twofold challenge with these client-initiated requests. First, it's important to be rigorous and systematic to be sure that the analysis is accurate and objective. Second, it's important to be diplomatic with clients who are likely to see limited value in a front-end analysis because they are in a hurry and are convinced there is no need to gather information about the problem. Dealing with these dual demands is challenging but doable.

Think About This

As an internal performance consultant, one of the best ways to deal with the need to gather data (and clients who think they have all the data you need) is to apologetically claim that it's organizational policy to gather certain data (that is part of a front-end analysis). Bureaucracy is a scapegoat that managers are all too familiar with. Therefore, if you blame the bureaucracy, managers will be much more obliging about allowing you to expand your information search.

Being Quick and Thorough

One criticism that many HRD professionals unfamiliar with HPI have is that it takes too long and doesn't work when you're in a hurry. Nothing could be further from the truth. The HPI process does not need to be slow, and there are plenty of examples of how a performance consulting approach can lead to a solution quicker than attempting to implement a training course or some other approach.

Basic Rule 35

A rigorous and objective performance analysis is not incompatible with quickness.

Front-end analysis work can be sped up to appeal to more clients and consultants who feel it moves too slowly. Most front-end analysis work actually moves faster (and identifies quicker solutions) than designing a training course (not to mention actually applying classes or seminars). Additionally, there are several techniques to do front-end analysis work quickly (Rossett, 1998).

Make the Purpose Clear

The single best approach for shortening the time and effort required of the front-end analysis is to know what the focus is on. In other words, the engagement or project alignment phase with the client is critical to speed up the analysis process.

Think About This

When a request from a client comes in, one way to get clarity on the purpose is to then go to the client's manager or the person above the client who owns the process or result. This is one way of minimizing the chance that the client will present a moving target that shifts during the analysis phase. Use the client's manager to help pin down the area of focus at the beginning of the process.

Hone in on Critical Information Resources

Rather than interview everyone on a team, identify the two or three critical performers. Instead of talking individually to everyone on the management team, invite them to a meeting to get all their input at once and then move on to the next area of research.

Think About This

New performance consultants find it easy to fall victim to analysis paralysis—seeking too much information and coping with uncertainty by asking for even more information. Don't seek scientific certainty or to establish causality with data. Get information from several different levels including, but not limited to, exemplars.

Tap Into Existing or Previous Data

Smart performance consultants avoid duplicating work by applying information from other projects that are relevant to the current task. For instance, previous work with the client's department (such as a facilitated meeting or a different performance issue six months ago) provides a head start with the information-gathering step.

Think About This

Prior training can be a wonderful source of client information that may shorten the time required for a front-end analysis. Offer to facilitate strategic planning sessions for various departments as a great way of getting access to information proactively.

Use Interventions as Information-Gathering Tools

In some cases, a client may insist upon immediate action. Given that most problems involve a range of solutions, early interventions can be used as information-gathering tools to shore up the interventions to follow.

Think About This

Just because the client calls it training doesn't mean that's all it has to be. Use the class breaks to strike up conversations with participants and interactive pieces to solicit issues. Through class structure, allow the participants to identify performance issues on their own. If it's done right, one pilot program can generate a tremendous amount of analytical data that can then be useful should you do an HPI project with those workers again.

Give Clients Something to React To

Rather than asking open-ended questions (which are less likely to lead to a limited or shorter answer), be willing to provide an example and have clients react to the example. This approach speeds up interviews and focus groups.

Think About This

Instead of asking such questions as "What is the cause?" or "Is there a better way to do this?" the performance consultant should provide something specific to react to. Show a performer a process and ask if it's too cumbersome. Hypothesize a particular cause and then ask the manager what data can prove or disprove that hypothesis. Describe a particular intervention and ask the client what issues would affect successful implementation. All of these queries provide specific reactions and speed up the information-gathering process.

It's critical to recognize that some of the most important data gathered by performance consultants during front-end work comes from omission. Smart performance consultants pay attention to what people say or do—and also to things they don't. Clients can't be expected to know the answer or provide the solution. Performance consultants have to acquire insight by seeing what the clients don't see. This may come from acts of omission, such as processes missing key steps, feedback systems that don't allow for customer feedback, or employees who praise the organization but never mention their manager.

Data-Collection Methods

Data is collected with either a front-end analysis or as part of the evaluation process. Common data-collection methods are discussed in the following sections.

Surveys

With the widespread use of email, the use of surveys as a data-collection tool in performance analysis has increased in viability. Email or Web-based surveys are now very common tools. Surveys can also be an invaluable method of data collection given how geographically dispersed many organizations are as well as the increasing use of shift work (and a 24/7 workforce). As a general rule, though, keep surveys simple. Too many questions will discourage some key resources from taking the time to respond to the survey.

Noted

A pollster or scientist would be worried about sample size and response rate with a survey. Performance consultants should not have these concerns. Remember, performers' responses are not the answer, but a performance consultant will view what respondents say critically. Just because 98 percent of the workforce says the problem is slow computers doesn't mean that the computers are the cause—that's only their perception of the cause.

Think About This

Use surveys to encourage participation as a way of reducing resistance to change. By sending out a short email survey to everyone, all will feel that their opinion counts (even though many of them won't respond anyway).

Focus Groups

Focus groups are a common means of getting input on training or other organizational concerns. There is value in using focus groups as a performance consultant.

However, beware of over-reliance on this source of information. Focus groups can be useful ways of gathering data quickly but may also make it difficult for individuals to open up within the group, especially if the reactions vary from their peers in the focus group.

Noted

Focus groups can be an excellent means of using the comments of one or two performers to provide some synergy and cueing. As Jane says something, it may spark an insight from Ralph. This is both a positive and a negative aspect to this data-collection method. Cueing, whereby one person's comment elicits a response from another, can also create peer pressure. Just because five of the six group members have a particular take on an issue doesn't mean that it's right.

Sometimes clients may insist that the performance consultant talk to everyone. Consider using focus groups when there are a lot of people who need to be contacted face-to-face for political reasons (and you don't think talking to everyone will provide valuable information). While this approach will help deal with political issues, it isn't likely to generate lots of high-value input from the participants. In such instances, a smart performance consultant might use the focus groups for a quick scan to identify performers that might be worth talking to individually in follow-up sessions.

Interviews

Interviews are a prime means of gathering data (for analysis or evaluation). Interviews have a significant advantage over surveys and focus groups in that the performance consultant can combine confidentiality with the ability to follow up responses and probe deeper. Interviews continually serve as sources of unexpected gems of information and are well worth the investment of time.

Observation

Trainers often get used to asking clients what they want and then providing it. This seems like good customer service and assumes the client knows best. However,

Noted

Interviews generally raise confidentiality issues. In order to ensure confidentiality, appropriate interview space is critical. While most organizations will provide a private office for interviews, this means leaving the performer's work space, often causing reluctance among managers about having their top performer leaving his or her work. So the interview needs to be work friendly, and performance consultants need to be wary that the manager doesn't shunt the weakest performers in for interviews (instead of their exemplars) to avoid taking top performers off the job.

Think About This

Smart performance consultants are flexible with interviews—they never go in with a rigid script. It makes sense to go in with a plan (and partial lists of questions), but smart consultants let the interview responses provide clues on additional things to ask. A smart way to conclude is with an open-ended question: "Is there anything else you think I should know?" That question often elicits some very useful details.

clients don't always know the answer or they are at times unwilling to share answers. Consequently, observation becomes a critical means of gathering data. Oftentimes, performers are so familiar with a job that some parts of the work process become subconscious, and they no longer notice what they do and, thus, are unable to describe it. Plus, there are always challenges with self-assessment and self-reporting (when asking performers to talk about their performance). Thus, observation may be the only way to catch elements that lead to poor or outstanding performance.

Document Review/Extant Analysis

Organizations are drowning in records and archives. Despite the dawn of the electronic age, paper has proliferated to the point that extant analysis can easily lead to paralysis analysis (where so much time is spent reading that time runs out and the project is never completed). Additionally, for legal reasons, many organizations will

Noted

There are a host of potential areas to focus on with observation. Is the sequence of tasks in the correct order? What changes has the performer made that appear to improve things? Has the performer adapted the tools, brought in his or her own tools, or developed any job aids? What aspects of the work appear awkward? How is the work flow? Are there bottlenecks or slack periods? To what extent does the way the work is actually done deviate from or align with the official process? What elements of the work allow for or require a lot of deviation versus tasks that require a uniform approach?

Think About This

The Hawthorne effect occurs when people are aware they're being observed—causing a change in their behavior. Despite the best efforts to be out-of-the-way as observers, performance consultants can't escape this issue. Instead of trying to remain inconspicuous, ask the performer questions, ask for an explanation on how something works, or even offer to play a role (such as operate the PowerPoint show for a sales presentation before clients). Performers are more likely to focus on performing when the performance consultant has some other role than that of a "just pretend I'm not here" observer.

be leery of releasing particular documents. Despite these limitations, extant analysis is a powerful data-gathering tool for performance consultants.

The key is to be very focused and narrow in the documents used in the extant analysis. Smart performance consultants identify a few key documents and draw the line so as to prevent overreading.

Basic Rule 36

Be selective with extant analysis. Don't fall victim to information overload. Identify key documents or material likely to have key information, and stick to those.

The documents used for extant analysis depend greatly upon what is available, the nature of the organization, and the type of performance issue. As a general rule, strategy plans and annual reports are good ways to verify business goal issues. Reports, memos, or even flipcharts from debriefs can be incredibly invaluable because they are likely to summarize lessons learned from a particular activity. Policy and procedure manuals or process documents can also be useful when combined with focus groups or interviews. The key to document review is to be selective in the material you use and not to go overboard.

Think About This

Extant analysis often works well in combination with observation or interviews. Get documentation on the official work process or the organization's description of the performer's role or position, and then compare what the document says to what is observed. Or, ask the performer to react to the document and identify what needs to change or what's outdated in the description.

External Benchmarking

External benchmarking is the process of gathering data from companies outside the client's organization. From a quality perspective (where the external benchmarking concept first emerged), this process can be very laborious and extensive. The HPI process often uses external benchmarking or baselining for limited purposes. Typically, benchmarking is used to document processes or establish targets for performance. This

Noted

One of the challenges with external benchmarking is that some companies will be reluctant to share information or it may be time consuming to gain access to that organization. However, this assumes a level of benchmarking beyond what most performance consultants probably need to do.

approach can be useful, especially if there doesn't seem to be any exemplars within the client's organization, or the performance process being evaluated is so broken that it's necessary to go outside to define a reasonable goal. Benchmarking can also be effective if the client is setting new targets or goals that the company has never pursued before.

Think About This

To gain information about how other companies do things, you can check with professional societies, which often collect "best of breed" or industry data as a resource.

With any data-collection effort, there is the question of confidentiality. Before using any data-collection method, it's important to reach an agreement with the client about access to information. Specifically, how confidential will any data be once gathered by the performance consultant? Confidentiality is critical for many performers to open up, and thus is an issue that must be addressed before going forward with serious data-collection efforts. For example, one performance consulting project was held up because the client (a public sector organization) was afraid that the report might be derogatory toward management and that the public could gain access to the performance consulting report through the state's freedom of information laws. Once the consultant and senior management were able to come to an understanding about limiting access to the report (by filing it as proprietary information), the project was then able to proceed.

Think About This

If concern exists that management will demand to see notes or surveys after confidentiality has been promised, there are several options. Try using a personal shorthand so that your notes aren't easily readable by others. Transcribe and compile all surveys onto a master sheet so nothing can be traced back to the author and destroy the originals. Additionally, stress to management that the findings are the insights of the consultant, not a summary report of what workers have said.

Discussing Performance Issues With Clients

Clients tend to contact performance consultants with specific interventions in mind. How can the consultant move a client from a transactional mode, in which the emphasis is on requests and filling them, to a performance focus? It's not easy.

First, it's important to keep in mind the advice of Dana Robinson on these matters. She likes to say, "You don't tell someone to perform, you ask them" (Willmore, 2002). Stated otherwise, strategies that involve debating or lecturing a client are doomed to failure. Remember, clients are convinced that they understand the problem better than performance consultants do. Convincing the client they are wrong is an uphill battle.

Instead, start at the level of conversation that the client is at. If the client is focused on a specific solution, then start there. If the client is dwelling on behavior, begin the conversation with that. After several minutes of conversation at that level, it's then time to segue the conversation to business objectives and strategic priorities. That way, the performance consultant can determine the critical performance.

Think About This

Here are some ways to shift the conversation from the client's transactional focus to a more business-focused perspective:

- "I'd like some context on these performers. What goals are they accountable for this year?"
- "And your hope is that with this training, these performers will be able to do what?"
- "Help me understand your priorities—what are the two or three biggest objectives in your department/team?"

Basic Rule 37

Most trainers are expected to provide what the client asks for—this is a transactional approach. As a performance consultant, it's important to help the clients, sometimes in spite of themselves. That means finding ways to deal with incorrect or premature requests.

When the client does not want to consider other options and the consultant is not in a position to demand more time to study the problem, what is the best way to proceed? Fortunately, there are a range of strategies to help move the client from a transactional focus to a performance focus (Willmore, 2002). None of these strategies is ideal, but they do address the reality of an imperfect world. If a client is dictating a solution and it isn't possible to say no, then one of the three approaches described here is likely to be an effective way to convert a likely failure to a possible success.

Foot in the Door

With this strategy, the performance consultant agrees to the client request, and then proceeds to gather information assuming that the client is correct. But, if the information the performance consultant gathers proves the client's request is inappropriate, now armed with data and rapport that she didn't have when the client first called, our performance consultant approaches the client about reconsidering the proposal. If the information justifies the client's original request (the client was right), then the consultant proceeds onward. This strategy works because when the client initially contacts the performance consultant, the consultant has no credibility or data to argue against the client's request. After agreeing to the client's request, the consultant has a chance to gather data and build rapport.

Noted

The "foot in the door" approach works best when the performance consultant has some time before implementing the client's request. This time allows for a front-end analysis and gives the performance consultant a chance to build credibility and rapport with the client.

What's in a Name?

This strategy involves coming up with a solution that addresses the actual problem, but it is called whatever the client requested. For instance, if a client asks for time management training (but it isn't possible to say "no" and it's clear that the problem actually involves various work procedures), then design a "training" class on time management that has participants in problem-solving groups to address those work procedures. Then, submit their recommendations to the client after the class.

This strategy is most effective when the client isn't micromanaging the intervention. This approach is efficacious if the client makes a fad request without knowing what it entails. For instance, team building means something different to practically everyone. A client can ask for a team-building intervention, and it could be just about anything. So instead of just cranking out a generic team-building retreat, have the team focus on analyzing performance issues within the organization and how to overcome those hurdles and call it team building.

Forest From the Trees

Sometimes it isn't possible to get out of doing what the client requests even though it's clear that the request is wrong or doomed to failure. The client may be so committed to doing that particular intervention that the performance consultant can use that commitment to get support for the correct solution as well. For instance, if the client is convinced that the way to improve performance is to bring in a motivational speaker, the performance consultant can convince the client that for the motivational speaker to be truly effective she also needs to do these other interventions (which will hit closer to the mark and have more impact). In this instance, it is recognizing the inevitable (the client's intervention can't be stopped) and using it as a way to shoehorn in solutions that will make a difference with the performance in question.

It's critical for performance consultants to be able to deal with the politics of client buy-in. Most of the time clients have their minds made up about what interventions to go with even before front-end analysis work has begun. An effective performance consultant develops strategies to gently move the client to the correct solution.

Noted

There will be plenty of times when a client reads a book or hears a speaker and insists that everyone in the company do the same. Or, maybe the client falls for a new fad. In any case, the performance consultant needs to identify what the real problem is and how to solve it. Then, the performance consultant needs to make the case to the client that for the speaker, book, or workshop to have any effect, other changes have to happen.

Getting It Done

The rigorous approach to analyzing performance gaps is what distinguishes HPI from many other approaches. HPI doesn't have to take a great deal of time, but it does require objectivity and a commitment to a process to avoid the misanalysis that is so common with other attempts to improve results.

Use exercise 6-1 to help you apply what's been covered in this chapter.

Exercise 6-1. Starting the HPI approach.

1. What requests for specific interventions do you get most commonly? Think about strategies or approaches for dealing with those requests that will allow you to transform the approach from transactional to a performance focus.

2. Do you get most of your work from certain clients representing specific offices or functions? If so, how can you proactively gather data on these clients so you already have some analysis information once they make a request?

3. Of the data-collection tools mentioned in this chapter, which approach do you have the least experience with? What could you do to build your competence with that data-collection tool?

(continued on page 106)

Exercise 6-1. Starting the HPI approach (continued).

4. What resources could you tap into to help with data collection so you can share the burden or automate some aspects?

5. What approaches can you think of for getting clients to be more open-minded in their requests for interventions?

6. Practice role playing a conversation with a hypothetical client. Have a spouse, friend, or peer play the role of client. Have the client start out with a request for a specific intervention for a specific group of performers. Practice gradually shifting the conversation from a focus on the intervention to performance outcomes and business objectives.

Once you've picked an initiative to deal with the performance gap, it's time to look at the design, delivery, and implementation of that solution. The next chapter in this book looks at the selection, design, and rollout of interventions.

7

Performance Consulting Solves Problems

 What's Inside This Chapter

Here you'll see how to:

▶ Choose and design the appropriate solution
▶ Partner to aid the design and rollout
▶ Identify common mistakes consultants make with design and implementation
▶ Implement effective change management strategies for generating cooperation with your solutions.

Taking Action

Trainers are knowledgeable about the design of interventions and their implementation. Some of that experience translates well to the needs of performance consulting. The primary differences are that a performance consultant will implement more than just training solutions and is likely to have to deal with multiple solutions for each problem. Many of the principles for designing and implementing training as well as HRD project management skills apply very well to performance consulting work in this part of the process.

Noted

Most performance gaps have multiple causes and, thus, require multiple solutions. Consequently, even though the work will be sequenced, most performance consultants will be involved with or manage several different solution projects for each performance gap.

Think About This

Because a performance consultant is capable of providing so many invaluable services, time becomes more valuable. And because there will likely be multiple solutions for each performance gap, it is less likely that the performance consultant will be able (or find it beneficial) to personally deliver or conduct many of the interventions. Performance consultants will want to focus on managing projects and delegating the actual design and delivery of many solutions to others or contractors.

Selecting the Right Solution

If the front-end analysis was done correctly, then choosing the right intervention is usually easy. A good front-end analysis will identify the root cause (or causes) of the performance gap. For example, if the root cause falls into the category of knowledge and skills, then the solution will come from the range of knowledge or skill interventions (such as classroom training, job aids, on-the-job training, or hiring people who already have the necessary skills). Front-end analyses that are rushed or incomplete lead to much more time investment in choosing and designing the interventions.

Basic Rule 38

The root cause dictates the choice of solution to close the performance gap.

The basic potential root causes can be categorized into six categories, or boxes, as mentioned in chapter 5 (Sanders & Thiagarajan, 2002):

- ▶ structure/process
- ▶ resources
- ▶ information
- ▶ knowledge/skills
- ▶ motives
- ▶ wellness.

Every root cause falls into one of these categories, and there are families of interventions that apply to each root cause category. This method of organization makes it possible to see common threads that run through root causes (such as a lack of knowledge and/or skills) and how the root cause links to a family of interventions.

Let's look at the knowledge/skills root cause category for some examples of this approach. Possible root causes that could fall under this category are the following:

- ▶ doesn't know how to do the work
- ▶ doesn't know when to use the skills (judgment and application)
- ▶ applies the skills in the wrong sequence
- ▶ used to know how, but lack of use leads to rust or retention problems.

These are just some of the possible root causes that fall within the scope of knowledge and skill.

Think About This

Most of the literature in the HRD field uses the term *intervention*. The term is a medical one that came from the early practitioners in the OD field. It makes much more sense when talking with clients to refer instead to solutions, actions, or recommendations.

To understand motivation and performance, it's important to recognize that clients have a tendency to view this issue as a lack of motivation to do good work. This is a simplistic analysis that provides little insight into how to improve the performance. Motivation isn't like a light switch that is turned on or off. Performers are always motivated—they just might not be motivated by the same things management would prefer them to be motivated by. Examples of root causes that fall under the motives category include the following:

▶ *Counter-rewards or counter-incentives:* There are plenty of instances where organizations pay lip service to a particular goal but actually provide incentive for other results. For instance, many call centers claim that outstanding customer service is one of their goals but then punish center staff for calls over 90 seconds in length. To keep calls short, staff sacrifice customer service, thus producing a negative effect, further hurting the chances of meeting the organizational goal.

▶ *Misguided incentive systems:* This is where a reward system has an effect counter to what it's intended to produce. A salesforce may receive most of their pay through sales bonus (commission). To close sales (and get higher bonuses), they make promises that operations and maintenance cannot keep (causing a sales decrease and a plummet in customer satisfaction).

▶ *Lack of appreciation:* Too many performers feel that good work isn't appreciated (and bad work isn't noticed). They reach a point where they feel unappreciated by management or co-workers and performance drops.

▶ *Competing motives:* Competing motives happen in almost every workforce; but because they tend to be covert, management is often oblivious to them. For instance, organizations offer bonuses for greater production but co-workers may resent having someone outperform them (and thus raise expectations). To fit in and avoid being ostracized by co-workers, performers may not perform to their best.

▶ *Residual effects of organizational deficiencies:* If the organization has serious or repeated deficiencies in areas like understaffing, poor tools, management failure to share information, or difficult working conditions, then over time these deficiencies are perceived as organizational apathy, which hinders motivation.

Physical resources get blamed for many performance issues. Most clients take a very simplistic view of this root cause issue. Too many clients will oversimplify the problem by arguing that if they only had more staff or more funding the problem would be solved. Typically, though, this involves throwing resources at a problem. Without further analysis, this is a wasteful approach. Physical resources involve all

Think About This

Often, what gets labeled as a morale problem is really a case of the organization's failure to keep promises or a case of difficult working conditions for performers. Over time, this can lead to lower motivation. Management then comes to the conclusion that they want to raise morale, but this misses the point—the problem isn't morale. The focus is the lowered motivation, which, in this case, the root cause is the organization's failure to keep promises to employees.

of the tangible assets and support that performers need. The term *tools* may conjure up pictures of wrenches, hammers, and drill bits, but white-collar workers have tools too. Issues such as outdated software, systems that crash, sufficient meeting space, enough time to do the work required can all be physical resource issues. Some examples of physical resource root causes are

- ▶ inappropriate or inferior tools and equipment (this is especially true for computers that are out-of-date or incompatible)
- ▶ problems with the work area and environment (such as a team that is geographically dispersed throughout the building)
- ▶ competition for scarce resources (which can lead to turf wars)
- ▶ poorly allocated resources (there is enough to go around but it's cumbersome to gain access or the resources are assigned to the wrong areas leading to bottlenecks)
- ▶ unachievable deadlines for the work.

Think About This

If a client insists that the root cause is related to resources, confirm that all employees do or do not reach the same accomplishment levels. Assume that all performers have the same resources. If you find one or more exemplars—or if there are significant gaps between performers—then performance can probably be improved with existing resource levels.

Noted

Be especially suspicious when clients blame physical resources for performance gaps. This is because many clients will view this as an opportunity to push their budget or pet projects (such as new computers for the team or changing the office furnishings or getting additional staff).

Structure and process encompass a huge and fertile area for root causes to performance gaps. Anything involved with company policy, the mission, how work is done, support processes (such as hiring, assessment, and benefits administration), or work roles comes into play here. Organizational structures that encourage silos (and thus prevent clear handoffs while minimizing information and resource sharing) are an example of structure/process issues. Some examples of structure/process root causes are

- political squabbling (where the organization is designed to promote division)
- unclear reporting relationships (who owns key decisions or processes is unclear, often caused by fuzzy lines of authorization)
- lack of accountability (work lacks measurable outcomes or some individuals are not responsible for their results)
- poorly designed processes (either inconsistent or missing key steps, or there could be a lack of agreement on the best way to do a function)
- illogical work sequence (this happens frequently when the client is used to slapping Band-Aid solutions on problems)
- unclear mission or direction (if performers don't display initiative, the first issue is whether they have a sense of purpose or priorities).

Because of the tendency to throw training at most performance issues, many organizations don't clearly understand how information contributes to performance gaps. Some root causes that get labeled as training problems are really information related. If this is a case where employees are able to do the job right some of the time or they used to be able to do the job, then it's not about knowledge or skills. Some examples of root causes in the information category are

- feedback (managers should provide timely, accurate feedback so that the performers have a clear sense of what was right or wrong, and outline expectations)

Think About This

When clients blame structure or process, they may have a tendency to phrase it in terms of their preferred solutions. For instance, in response to a question about why reports are late, a client might say, "If we saved the content review until after the draft is finished it would be completed on time." The problem with this analysis is that it pushes a solution (change when we review the draft). Consequently, resist phrasing the root cause in terms of what should be done.

- conflicting information (policies may have changed over time or explanations of what to do in particular situations may be contradictory)
- late or delayed information
- exclusion from critical information or failure to be informed.

The work culture within North America has tended to emphasize a stoic nature and a belief that while at work it's important to leave your personal life at home. More recently, analysis of workplace issues has recognized that wellness (physical and emotional health) has a tremendous impact on performance. There are a number of root causes within the wellness category:

- physical capacity (unable to perform either because of injury or the job requires strength or height the performer lacks)
- emotional or mental problems (this includes things like attention deficit disorder [ADD], depression, or distraction by marital problems at home)
- substance abuse (such as alcohol or drugs)
- poor health (a parent of a young child who consequently catches lots of colds from the child or suffers from sleep deprivation because the child isn't sleeping through the night)
- shift demands (the stress of the workday or fatigue from a long shift may reduce performance as the day goes on).

Families of Interventions

With a better understanding of the root cause categories, it's important to see how these root cause categories link to possible interventions and also examples of the kinds

Think About This

If wellness is a possible factor, the issue of evaluation timing is critical. For example, some seasons are more conducive to disease (such as the flu or colds), or some performers may do well at the beginning of the workday but become stressed and fatigued by the end of the day when performance declines. Therefore, when the measurement or observation takes place is a critical factor with assessing wellness issues.

of solutions that fall into each intervention category. It's time to look at knowledge/skills, information, motivation, resources, structure/process, and wellness solutions.

Basic Rule 39

Many trainers feel intimidated by the range of possible solutions available to performance consultants. Don't be. Performance consultants are not expected to be an expert in all or even most of these options. Performance consultants need to be able to identify when a particular solution would solve a problem—not how to design and deliver each particular remedy.

There is a diverse list of possible options for addressing knowledge/skills deficiencies. Some possible examples include

- traditional, instructor-led, classroom training
- action-learning groups
- on-the-job training
- a change in recruiting practices (so instead of hiring performers who need to be trained to do the job, people who already have the correct skills are hired)
- e-learning or self-paced instruction options
- job aids
- electronic performance support systems (EPSS) or even automation of some jobs (so that it isn't necessary to staff those positions)
- job redesign (so that skills the performers lack are no longer required for that job).

Performance consultants are able to choose the right options from this list by using the root cause analysis. For instance, if a group forgets how to do a particular task that is rarely used yet critical (such as how to operate a fire extinguisher in case of an electrical fire), a job aid is the most effective means of dealing with knowledge problems due to memory loss. Thus, using the root cause to select the right solution leads to clearer and more effective choices for performance solutions.

Think About This

In many knowledge and skills situations, a job aid provides the best ROI (combination of results and low cost).

As work becomes more complex and the world changes at a quicker pace, information becomes crucial. This is in part because it's easy for it to get outdated and because it's easy for it to become distorted in a large organization with dispersed networks. Although there are a multitude of possible information interventions, some examples are

- competency models (to identify the key tasks for a job or what best practices are)
- feedback and appraisals (so employees have a better sense of priorities and performance accuracy)
- conflict management (when anger or conflict serves as a barrier to information dissemination)
- IT networks (to speed up communication)
- newsletters (to provide companywide access to information).

Think About This

Information needs to be judged by the impact on performance, not the activity. Performers are the best judge of the quality of the information. If they're still confused about priorities or what management expects of them, then the information (about priorities or expectations) is inadequate.

Many clients tend to view motivational interventions as falling into three options: motivational speakers, changing formal benefits, or making threats of some kind. The range of potential motivation solutions is far more sophisticated than those simple options. Some examples of possible motivation solutions are

> ▸ feedback processes (so performers have a better sense of what is important and feel valued)
> ▸ mission clarification (so priorities and purpose are clearer)
> ▸ reorganization (to change office norms and alter peer dynamics)
> ▸ cafeteria plans (to provide a better fit between company benefits and individual needs)
> ▸ employee involvement systems (to stimulate creativity and ideas from the workforce)
> ▸ customer interaction (so employees see directly what a difference their performance makes).

Noted

Motivation interventions cover an incredibly diverse range of options because the reasons someone is motivated to behave or perform a particular way will vary from performer to performer. It's critical when dealing with a motivation root cause to avoid oversimplification.

Structure and process involve two very different sets of issues that both deal with the design of the organization and how things are done. Among the possible structure/process interventions are

> ▸ process mapping (to identify redundancies and bottlenecks)
> ▸ strategic planning and visioning (to set resource priorities and determine direction of the organization)
> ▸ revising policies and procedures (to eliminate counterproductive rules and enable particular kinds of behaviors)
> ▸ changing reporting and lines of authority (to speed up communication and clarify accountability)
> ▸ defining work roles (to eliminate overlap and close gaps)
> ▸ partnering agreements (to quickly add resources or manage expectations).

Think About This

OD consultants can be tremendous assets in structure interventions. Quality control experts or Six Sigma Black Belts can be very helpful during process solutions. Look to use them on design and implementation of interventions in these areas.

Resource root causes typically involve areas that many trainers feel inexperienced with. After all, how many times do most trainers make recommendations about work clothing or furniture? Unless the trainer is involved in specialized courses (such as safety, IT, or technical training), these topics generally involve subject matter expertise outside of the training experience. Yet resources are a critical category and one that performance consultants will likely want to partner with others in the organization to develop specifics on each solution required to close the performance gap. Examples of some resource interventions include

- ▶ changing space layout (to promote team communication by putting team members closer together and knocking down walls)
- ▶ providing a new tool or job aid
- ▶ improving the phone system to provide alternatives for customers calling in and decrease wait time
- ▶ scheduling access to limited resources (such as the conference room) so others aren't shut out and unable to use it
- ▶ giving employees company credit cards (so they can buy needed supplies immediately)
- ▶ providing cross-training so personnel can shift to other roles when bottlenecks occur and avoid lags in cycle time.

Noted

Don't automatically assume that a resource intervention involves spending more money. Many good solutions in this area will involve using existing resources in a more coherent fashion. These opportunities can be identified by analyzing work processes and workflow to see where bottlenecks occur and where slack resources are at given times.

Wellness issues can run the gamut from illegal behavior like substance abuse to challenges that appear much more trivial (employees get tired and grumpy at the end of their shift) yet still equally impact performance. Examples of wellness solutions to address performance gaps include

- ▶ work environment improvements (to improve air quality and decrease noise)
- ▶ changing break schedules (so employees remain focused and refreshed during the most stressful periods of their work)
- ▶ setting up e-learning opportunities or night courses so performers working on the night shift don't have to come in during their sleep time to attend training
- ▶ coaching staff members on how they deal with conflict and differences (to decrease tension and stress within the office)
- ▶ stressing preventive maintenance and encouraging physical fitness (to reduce absenteeism and health-care costs).

Noted

Wellness interventions are especially workable in individual or team settings where it's possible to tailor solutions to a limited group.

The examples of interventions discussed so far in this chapter are just that—examples. The actual list of possible performance solutions is nearly endless and limited only by the creativity of the performance consultant.

In some cases the line between intervention categories (such as wellness and motivation, or motivation and resources) may get fuzzy. This is because this process categorizes interventions by the root cause category. Use a team-building intervention as an example. It could fall under knowledge/skills (if the team is failing because the members don't know how to collaborate well), motivation (if members have no confidence in one another), information (if there are internal silos that prevent quick communication), or structure/process (if the office is failing because it is too rigid and a team-based structure will speed up work). Don't get hung up on the boundaries. The primary purpose for categorizing interventions is so that root cause analysis drives the solution selection.

Synergy Among Solutions

You'll often have multiple root causes for a performance gap. Look for synergies among possible solutions. See table 7-1 for an example.

Table 7-1. Finding synergetic interventions.

Root Cause Category	Root Cause	Possible Interventions
Knowledge/Skills	Doesn't know how to apply skills in the right sequence	• On-the-job training • Job aids • Coaching
Motives	Rewarded for working slowly because fast work results in heavier workload	• Change rewards • Change workload • Coaching
Structure/Process	Fails to adapt work process to unique situations	• Workflow analysis • Coaching • Clearer policy

Even though there are three different root causes in three different categories, a possible solution for each root cause involves coaching. The point is not that coaching solves all problems, only that many times it is possible to use one intervention to solve several performance gaps. A wise performance consultant will always look for possible synergies among solutions.

Factors to consider in selecting and implementing solutions are numerous. Sequencing is an important one. Recommending a series of solutions to a client—all of which will need to start at the same time and use the same resources—is poor planning. For complex performance issues involving a range of interventions, a wise performance consultant will want to consider a range of options that deal with different resources and timeframes so the solutions don't strain key performers or create massive bottlenecks.

 Noted

It is likely that a performance consultant (either internal or external) will be managing several different projects dealing with several different performance issues in the same timeframe. Therefore, ideal approaches to project management are likely to be replaced by more pragmatic needs of scheduling activities and steps when the time is available.

Examples of some considerations to keep in mind when selecting groups of solutions are

▶ *Timing:* Are there work cycles that dictate when it's appropriate to implement activities? For instance, major initiatives for an accounting firm around tax time would constitute poor timing.

▶ *Resource demands:* Whose participation is needed, and what performers must be involved? What resources can the organization commit to the solution? A mentoring program in which the top sales staff work with new hires may be fine theoretically but unrealistic for an organization that can't afford to take its best salespeople away from the job.

▶ *Location:* Does everyone need to be together or can this be done dispersed? As general rule, pilot projects are best done far from corporate headquarters (to minimize interference and meddling by senior management).

▶ *Sequencing:* Which solutions need to come first? What actions can be made to gain support for the project? It may be easier to develop and deliver the training, but it won't be as effective until the appropriate support systems (new appraisal systems and an improved work process that utilizes the new skills) are in place.

Basic Rule 40

A wise performance consultant always gives the client two options for each performance issue. The performance consultant may have a strong opinion about what solution is best but should always give the client a choice. The client may know information he or she cannot share with the consultant that affects the intervention selection (such as certain players are going to be fired, there will be a merger, or there are new product rollouts that will require certain resources).

Job Aids

Technically speaking, job aids are a part of the knowledge/skills intervention series. A job aid provides direction and demonstrates various processes or functions to performers. It's worth mentioning job aids separately because they often have such an incredibly high ROI compared with many other interventions.

Job aids can run the gamut from a laminated pocket card with product specifications to a four-page preflight checklist for a pilot. Often, they are capable of providing knowledge or skills solutions to experienced workforces at substantially lower costs than other knowledge and skills interventions (such as classroom training, coaching, or e-learning).

One of the lessons that job aids offer about intervention selection is this: Don't just pick a solution that addresses the problem, look for the best solution. What constitutes "best" varies given the criteria used. In some cases, the best solution is the one that fits the internal culture or politics of the organization. In other instances, two solutions may both solve the problem but one particular option is much cheaper than the other—thus offering a much higher ROI.

Once an intervention category is identified, compare several possible solutions to see which one has the best ROI. There might be substantially different ROIs for a training class depending upon whether internal trainers are used versus contractors. Once an intervention category is identified, examine different solutions within that category to select the ones with the highest ROI for the client.

Noted

Wise performance consultants place a great deal of emphasis on managing client expectations at every stage of the HPI process (a big change if you are used to operating as a trainer).

The Design and Development Process

Once the performance consultant has identified the relevant solutions and gotten client support, the focus shifts to the design and development of whatever interventions are required to close the performance gap. There are several basic steps to the design and development process.

> ► *Clarify the intervention's objectives:* It's critical that the performance consultant and the client are clear about what the intervention needs to achieve. Because this may involve several solutions to deal with one performance gap, each solution might not have the same objectives. It is also important to determine the mandatory features to each solution and the desirable (but not essential) elements to avoid.

Noted

Specifying the objectives for each solution is critical for both the design phase and managing client expectations. Learning objectives should have three components (Mager, 1984):

- Performance result: *the desired outcome for the performer*
- Conditions: *the circumstances the performer will need to be able to do this work*
- Standards: *the level of performance required for the work.*

For instance, someone attending a presentation skills course might be expected to achieve the following learning objective: Prepare a 10-minute PowerPoint presentation with no errors and consistent with company logo policy in less than 30 minutes using a company-issued PC and software. This learning objective has all three components: performance result, conditions, and standards.

▶ *Create a detailed design plan:* The design plan is the roadmap for how to move from concept (the intervention idea) to actual solution prototype (the pilot program ready to test). This involves a series of steps (including identifying subject matter experts, gathering data, developing a structure for the intervention, and analyzing the target population). The steps will vary somewhat depending on the nature of the intervention. For instance, an intervention that involves learning will have different design considerations from one that involves resources. Regardless of the intervention, it's critical to flesh out the details for what the solution will look like and what components will be part of it.

▶ *Assemble a development team:* For the performance consultant, almost all intervention design and development will be done as a team. Why operate this way—especially if the performance consultant has experience with the type of solution being designed? First, time is more valuable now as a performance consultant. The performance consultant should offload any instructional design duties to free up more time for analysis or evaluation work (or to manage other elements or solutions that are part of the larger project). Second, performance consultants deal with a wider range of potential solutions—many of which they won't have practical design experience with—so it makes sense to manage or advise on the design process but delegate the actual work to someone with expertise.

▶ *Develop a prototype and test it:*
Despite the client's insistence for
a solution, the performance consultant will want to first go with a
beta test, pilot program, or prototype. This is because in doing a
pilot program, valuable lessons
emerge that can avoid wasted
resources. It's important to avoid
studying things to death. Instead,

Think About This

Regardless of how experienced the performance consultant is with the solution
being developed, it's always helpful to
create the design with multiple people to
bounce ideas off one another.

the prototype may actually show ways to shorten the intervention or speed up
implementation. It can also result in goodwill, which is helpful in marketing
the solution and getting people to accept it.

▶ *Plan and roll out the intervention:* Assume the pilot program is done and
there is feedback that has identified ways to tweak the intervention and
improve it. Now it's time for the implementation. If the solution needs to be
applied multiple times (as would be the case for a large group of performers),
then there are roll-out and implementation issues. Some of the issues to consider include barriers to change and what resistance is reasonable to expect. It
is also critical to identify what other systems and policies are inconsistent
with the change.

Basic Rule 41

An effective performance consultant always seeks to partner—or
establish collaborative relationships—with people throughout the
performance consulting process. This is especially true with the element
of intervention design and implementation.

Common Mistakes

There are four main errors that performance consultants often make with intervention selection, design, and implementation:

1. Failure to partner: Performance consultants who don't pull in other
   resources and engage clients to work together will fail.

Think About This

Sometimes the performance consultant is not the most credible person to be the visible advocate for the policy. Search out credible allies (this is where the partnering process can be especially valuable). Perhaps someone such as the union representative, a shop fore-man, or a well-respected performer could be a "public face" for the program by visiting worksites to explain the new intervention to gain support.

2. Failure to consider culture: Every organizational culture is different, so a solution that works in one company may flop in another because of the differences in internal culture.
3. Failure to manage change: Regardless of how good the implementation plan is, it will require adaptation as the process unfolds. There will always be unanticipated barriers and hidden opportunities.
4. Failure to adapt to the client: The performance consultant can only go as far as the client is willing to go, and pushing the client too far is unwise. Be willing to adjust to the limits of the client.

Although this is not a mistake per se (in the sense that it's wrong to do this kind of work), one frequent headache for many consultants is what is sometimes referred to as a "day one problem." With a day one problem, the performers have never been able to get it right or meet expectations. As a result, analysis is often problematic, and the performance consultant may choose to implement an intervention only to discover it reveals another underlying problem. When the second underlying problem is addressed, the consultant then discovers an even deeper issue. The consequence of a day one problem is that what initially appears to be a simple issue turns out to be a resource hole that sucks up time and money by the performance consultant before he or she can show meaningful results.

Change Management

Once the initial pilot program is complete and revisions are made, it's time to roll out the interventions and start dealing with change management—right? No. For the smart performance consultant, change management started as soon as he or she

Think About This

Even the most successful HPI projects can (and often) come perilously close to failure. The design and implementation stage is always fraught with potential disaster. Don't get too depressed when mistakes happen and don't get too confident that the design is flawless.

began work on the project. If the performance consultant starts focusing on change management once the solutions are ready to roll out, then it's too late in the process.

One key factor with managing change will be the organizational culture. All organizations have a series of unstated values, ways of interaction, informal rewards, symbols, and traditions that constitute the organizational culture. Understanding the organizational culture is critical, and failure to do so will likely doom information-gathering efforts and result in an intervention that the organization will find unacceptable.

Even internal performance consultants should never assume they've got a good handle on the culture at their organizations. The culture between corporate and field offices often varies dramatically. Also, the cultural variety between different functions (such as engineering and customer service) is often great.

Another key element in effective change management is the communication plan for the intervention. Find a way to let people know change is coming and then communicate to them what is at stake for them personally with this solution. There will be a host of issues, such as:

▶ Who is a credible voice for change and in dealing with the performers?
▶ What kinds of resistance and apathy need to be overcome?

Basic Rule 42

Change management runs through all elements of the HPI project from start to finish. Performance consultants should never stop looking for ways to provide a better fit between the solutions, the performers, and their organization.

▶ What else is going on in the organization that could interfere with this change effort?

▶ What have the performers' previous experiences been with change efforts?

One element of the change management process is to identify components of the system that are incompatible with the proposed solution. It's valuable to view this issue much as physicians view organ transplants. When a patient receives a new lung or kidney, the human body tends to resist the new organ, attacking it as if it were an infection. Therefore, health-care providers must work hard to make sure that the body does not reject the new organ. With an HPI initiative, the performance consultant will need to work hard to do just the same—make sure it is not rejected by the organization. This rejection can come from active resistance (from employees who think the new plan is a bad idea) or systems and processes that inadvertently undercut the intervention.

Getting It Done

This chapter focused on the selection and implementation of the solutions intended to close the performance gap. As a trainer you already have some experience with this by dealing with the design and implementation of training courses. But, as a performance consultant, the range of possible interventions you might deal with increases significantly.

This increases design complexity issues but should not intimidate you. Performance consultants are, for the most part, good generalists. You might view a performance consultant as a jack of all trades, because you will deal with many different interventions and aren't expected to be an expert in all of them.

Apply the information in this chapter to complete exercise 7-1.

Exercise 7-1. Designing and implementing interventions.

1. In what intervention areas do you have strong design and development skills? For those intervention categories you feel less confident with, what resources exist that you might tap into or partner with?

2. If there are no resources to partner with for particular interventions, begin assembling a list of specialists you can call upon as consultants for specific functions such as space planners, ergonomics specialists, facilitators, large group intervention specialists, strategic planners, process mapping specialists, instructional designers, graphic designers, and so forth.

3. What would you say is the prevailing culture at your organization (or if you're external, your primary client)? How does that culture differ throughout the organization (such as between headquarters and the field)? If you're not sure, how could you assess the organizational culture?

4. Identify a successful change effort with your organization or client. What was it about the design and implementation that made the change effort so successful? What lessons can you learn from this change effort?

5. Now identify an unsuccessful change effort within your organization or for a major client and ask yourself what contributed to its failure.

Evaluation is what allows you to improve your solutions and to determine how effective you've been in meeting organizational goals. Effective evaluation also provides the objective data that builds your credibility as a performance consultant. The next chapter takes a look at evaluation.

8

Evaluating Results: The Real Test of Performance

What's Inside This Chapter

Here you'll see how to:

▶ Do a formative and a summative analysis
▶ Make evaluation as simple and painless as possible
▶ Conduct an ROI analysis.

Conquering Evaluation

For most trainers, evaluation is a scary subject. Trainers tend to be wonderful at evaluating reactions (Kirkpatrick's level 1). But, push trainers to show quantitative results or business impacts and you're likely to hear any or all of these phrases:

▶ "Soft skills impacts just can't be evaluated."
▶ "It's so intuitive that learning is valuable, there is no need to try to see if it affects the bottom line."
▶ "We measure our performance; we average a 4.8 on a 5.0 scale based upon course attendee satisfaction!"

▶ "It's not possible to link training to results, so to demand anyone to show this is unreasonable."

▶ "Pushing evaluation is just another effort by bean counters to focus only on numbers and ignore the human side of organizations."

All these positions are nonsense. However, because so many trainers are paranoid about evaluation, it is a subject that most HRD professionals approach with trepidation. That's a pity because evaluation is fairly easy when done correctly. If a performance consultant follows the HPI process correctly, evaluation is quite simple.

Key Evaluation Principles

Just a couple of basic points regarding evaluation can make the process almost painless for performance consulting projects.

First, evaluation is a critical element of the HPI process. Without evaluation, it's not performance consulting. It is not something done just to justify the training budget or because the client demanded it. On the contrary, evaluation is a key element in tweaking and improving the solution to make it better. It is an essential part of decision making: There are probably several options to weigh before an intervention is implemented (for example, the decision about whether to use internal staff or external consultants). Evaluation informs those decisions. Performance consulting aims at helping the organization meet critical business goals, and evaluation determines if those business goals have been met. It doesn't matter what the client expects in terms of evaluation. Evaluation is not optional.

Basic Rule 43

Evaluation starts at the beginning. Don't wait until after the intervention to begin evaluating.

Most trainers are taught that evaluation is something that happens after the training is over. Waiting until after everything has happened to figure out the impact of the intervention is incredibly difficult. But, with performance consulting, evaluation starts at the very beginning of the process. The initial conversation about business goals with the client forms the basis for evaluation planning. When the client talks about critical objectives and the accomplishments that must be achieved, this conversation also provides the evaluation targets and measures of success. It's obvious that effective evaluation starts at the beginning of the HPI process.

Basic Rule 44

Always determine what the purpose for the specific evaluation is—what is the purpose of gathering the data? By answering this question, it will be clear what kind of evaluation is necessary and what the evaluation design needs to look like.

There is a tendency for some trainers to automatically gather certain kinds of data. There is even a drive within some organizations to adopt uniform evaluation forms and processes so questions are standardized among participants and within programs. This is a foolish approach.

Data should be collected because it suits a particular purpose or fills a specific need. Data on participant reactions is invaluable if the intent is to offer the course again, because you may want to revise and improve it. ROI data is useful to decide if the course was worth the investment. It's critical to always ask what the purpose of the evaluation is. By defining the purpose of the evaluation, it becomes clear what kind of data is relevant and which approach is best for conducting the evaluation.

Noted

Evaluate with rhyme and reason. If it's clear what the purpose of the data is (the purpose of the evaluation), then it will be obvious what kind of data to gather and how to evaluate it.

Here are three examples to clarify why it's critical to identify the evaluation purpose:

1. Pat is considering a team-building intervention for a troublesome team and, if it's successful, may try a similar intervention across the organization. He already knows that the team-building initiative is likely to be successful for

the specific team, but he needs to know if it makes sense to roll out this intervention across the organization. In this case, an ROI analysis fits the organization's needs because ROI data provides insight as to whether an organization-wide rollout is sensible.

2. Diane's organization is required to provide particular safety training by the state. She isn't allowed to alter the materials, the content, or the format. The training is not optional. In this case, asking participants for their reaction would be a waste of time because their reaction cannot lead to any changes. A level 4 or ROI analysis is a waste of time as well because the training is required by law; whether it is effective or nets a positive return is irrelevant.

3. Roger designed a job aid for the 5,000 sales associates in a department store chain. He then did extensive testing and solicited feedback. After this formative analysis, Roger made decisions on what the final job aid would look like. Then to save money, Roger produced all 5,000 job aids at once. If Roger is unwilling or unable to modify and reprint the job aid, it's foolish to solicit feedback from users because the input will not be used.

Basic Rule 45

The better defined business goals and performance accomplishments are for a project, the easier evaluation is because establishing clear business needs and determining performance drivers provides targets to measure against.

When the front-end analysis has clearly identified specific business goals and determined specific performance drivers, there are clear targets to measure against. This is one more illustration of the point that evaluation starts at the beginning of the HPI process. Work done at the beginning of the process in defining goals and targets is valuable later on when evaluating the impact of an intervention.

Types of Evaluation

There are a number of different approaches, methods, and models for evaluation. Several are described in the following sections.

The Five Levels of Evaluation

Donald Kirkpatrick's (1975) four levels is a commonly used approach toward training evaluation. Level 1 measures participant reaction. Level 2 focuses on skills or knowledge that participants learned. Level 3 looks at behavior change on the job. Level 4 assesses impact on the organization. Jack Phillips (1991) has added what is sometimes referred to as level 5, ROI.

The Kirkpatrick approach does not work effectively for nontraining solutions. If the intervention doesn't involve learning (such as upgrading computers or changing benefits or shortening a work process), then some of the levels don't apply. For instance, what is level 2 (skills learned) for a solution that involves clarifying a key policy or simplifying a work process? Furthermore, it's important to understand that the Kirkpatrick model does not show how to do evaluation—it's an evaluation typology, but it is a standard in the training field and is a common reference point for most HRD professionals when discussing evaluation. Whether using this approach or not, it's important for performance consultants to be familiar with Kirkpatrick's approach and terminology because many clients use it.

Basic Rule 46

A formative evaluation seeks to improve a solution. A summative evaluation determines the impact the solution had on the organization.

Formative Evaluation

Two other distinctions to clarify evaluation are the categories of summative and formative evaluation. Formative evaluation looks for ways to improve an initiative. A pilot program is a type of formative evaluation because the purpose of the pilot is to troubleshoot the program and determine how to improve it. Evaluations that seek feedback on how to improve materials or instructors are all elements of formative evaluations. The purpose of a formative evaluation is to get information to improve the intervention, meaning that if the solution is a one-time event or is mandated by law, it makes no sense even to ask some formative questions.

What is the process for doing a formative evaluation? An experienced trainer already has an idea of the answer to this question. Each formative analysis varies

Noted

Formative evaluations are common ways of improving interventions. They make sure the solution is well designed, meaning:

- *Does the intervention adhere to key design principles?*
- *Could it be more efficient?*
- *Does it do what it's supposed to do?*
- *Does it fit the user/audience/performer demographics?*
- *Does it fit the timing/sequence/design outline?*

according to the nature of the intervention being assessed. Common approaches include

- ▶ pilot or beta tests
- ▶ comparison to design principles or standards (For instance, how consistent is the course with the instructional systems design model?)
- ▶ use of subject matter experts (SMEs) to evaluate content
- ▶ level 1 analysis including postsession focus groups to solicit additional reactions.

It's critical with a formative analysis that the evaluation is conducted so there is sufficient time to utilize the information derived from it. If the formative evaluation stage asks for user feedback on materials but the results don't get back until the workbook is being printed, then it's too late. As a project manager and planner, the performance consultant needs to build formative analysis into the project in a logical timeframe.

Noted

Formative evaluation is not likely to be a one-time event with each intervention. It is common to have several stages during design, development, and rollout of an initiative for which formative data is gathered.

A performance consultant involved in the design of an e-learning course would typically seek formative evaluation data at several points during course development. Once there is a course template, it makes sense to seek user input for one module of the course before all of the modules are populated with content to avoid the situation where users find the design to be counterintuitive. It would be important to seek formative data on content accuracy once the course is complete. In addition, the designers would want to seek feedback from power users as well as technical or systems experts to see how the design and structure of the course might run into hardware or software issues. Consequently, formative evaluation is not something that is likely to occur just once in the measurement process.

Think About This

Level 1 data (participant reaction) is a powerful tool for formative evaluation.

Summative Evaluation

A summative analysis is an evaluation of the ultimate impact of an intervention. Wouldn't a formative evaluation do this? No. A formative evaluation might indicate that a time management course does indeed follow adult learning principles and the ADDIE instructional design process (Analyze, Design, Develop, Instruct, Evaluate) and confirm that participants did indeed learn the key course principles. But, a formative analysis cannot determine if performers became more productive or if the organization met its goals. A summative analysis focuses on levels 4 (impact on the organization) and 5 (ROI of the intervention).

It might be helpful to look at an example of a summative evaluation. Joe's Biometrics is a hypothetical company that makes medical instruments to measure bodily functions and vital signs. Management at Joe's Biometrics wants to increase sales of a new blood pressure monitor by 30 percent by next year. A performance consultant recommends the following initiatives:

1. Develop new job aids for the salesforce.
2. Provide Palm Pilots to the salespeople so they can access pricing and product information quickly in the field.
3. Provide coaching for sales staff with low close rates.

The summative impact of these interventions would involve determining how much sales went up in the next year and also an examination of ROI for these interventions. The summative data shows that the Palm Pilots did contribute to an increase in sales, but their cost was not worth their contribution to the overall sales increase. The summative evaluation would not be concerned with data on participant reactions (certainly they liked having the Palm Pilots) or learning (with the Palm Pilots, the salesforce became more technologically literate).

Does it make sense to do all four or even five levels of evaluation for most interventions? Doing so provides implied links from one level to the next. For instance, if participants liked the intervention, learned from it, behavior changed, and results improved, then there appears to be some degree of linkage between the intervention and the improvement in results. If the client is only interested in organizational results (a summative evaluation), then why evaluate reactions or learning? If the performance consultant is confident in the root cause analysis, then a connection between the result and the solution was established upfront. Thus, the implied link between participant reaction, learning, participant behavior, and organizational results obtained from doing all four or five levels would be less valuable. If some of the evaluation data will not be relevant or useful, then why collect that data?

Summative evaluation starts with a level 4 analysis. For it to be effective, there must be a pretty clear link between the solution and the business goal reflected in organizational results. The performance consultant must have confidence in the root cause analysis.

Summative evaluation looks at any impact on organizational results that can be attributed to the performance initiative (figure 8-1). If the results are positive, then the consultant might do a level 5 analysis to determine if the intervention was worth

Noted

For most line managers or executives, a summative analysis (at level 4 or level 5) is sufficient. They are interested in the results for the organization or business unit. Therefore, if there is a clear link in the root cause analysis to the performance and the performance to the business goal, clients are usually satisfied to see changes in the business results. The clear linkage at the front end of the process (in the analysis stage) usually reduces the burdens on the performance consultant in the evaluation stage.

Figure 8-1. ASTD's approach to summative analysis.

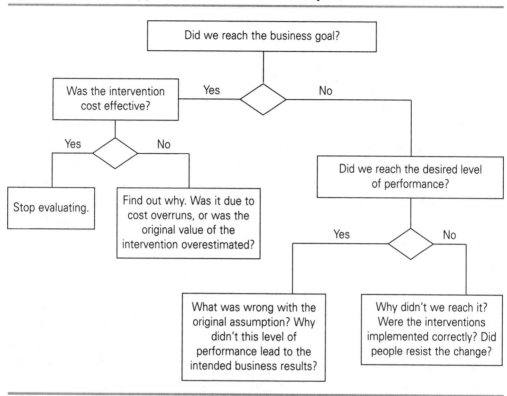

Source: Unpublished. Based on the "HPI in the Workplace" course. Alexandria, VA: ASTD.

the cost. If the results are positive or inconclusive (there was some limited change in results but it's difficult to assign those results to the solution), then it might make sense to do a level 3 evaluation (to see if performance has changed). That way, if it's difficult to show a link between the initiative and level 4 results (business goals), a stronger link to level 3 results (performance) can bolster the argument that the solution was still effective and either accounted for what increase in business results did happen or perhaps offset other factors (such as a declining economy that should have resulted in lower sales were it not for the performance initiative).

What to Measure

A good front-end analysis leads to clear business goals and key performance outcomes. If that's the case (and the root cause analysis shows a strong link between the

Think About This

The timing of an evaluation is a major consideration for performance consultants. For a trainer, it is easy to do level 1 evaluation immediately at the conclusion of the course; but if a performance consultant wants to measure the impact the course had on the organization, there must be sufficient time for the course to have an effect. The timing may be influenced by issues like seasons, market dynamics, or enough opportunities for the participants to apply the course material. For instance, if Joe's Biometrics conducts cardiopulmonary resuscitation training for all employees and then a month later checks to see what the level 4 impact is (how many lives were saved through cardiopulmonary resuscitation), the answer is likely to be zero. One month isn't enough time to likely have an opportunity for participants to apply the training to save any lives.

behavior in question, the performance accomplishment, and the business goal), then the key element to measure is the change in the business goal identified by the client.

Some clients or managers argue that this can't be done for their organization for various reasons. One argument is that the organization isn't a business because it's military, governmental, not-for-profit, and so on. Nonsense! The label *business goal* is generic business rather than a profit enterprise. One might say none of the goals can be quantified, and thus progress on the goals cannot be measured. This is usually wrong, because most organizations find value in:

- ▶ saving money
- ▶ less rework or less waste
- ▶ being more productive by producing more with less
- ▶ providing better service and getting happier, more satisfied customers
- ▶ reducing cycle time without sacrificing quality or increasing cost.

All these things can be measured. The issue is not whether something can be measured, because almost everything can be measured. The question is whether something is worth measuring.

Ideally, the focus for the evaluation is a business goal that is also a priority for the business. In this case, such a goal would probably already be supported by significant data collected by the organization, thereby simplifying some evaluation challenges.

Basic Rule 47

Always push a client to define a goal quantitatively. Most goals can be measured quantitatively, providing a way to gauge impact when evaluation of the results takes place.

At times, however, the business objective may be hard to measure. Examples of this are branding awareness, customer goodwill, enterprise resilience, and intellectual capital. Such targets may sound somewhat soft or hard to quantify. If an organization can't directly measure an objective, it is important to identify indicators for that objective. Indicators are factors that are associated with an outcome or result.

For example, the organization may wish to improve employee health to minimize health-care expenses in the long run. However, accurately monitoring employee health is difficult—it would likely involve violating employees' privacy. But, a possible indicator for employee health could be the number of sick days taken. This is not measuring health because some employees may call in sick if they want to take a day off or extend a vacation. On the other hand, some employees may show up sick to work because they can't afford to take the time off. But, the number of sick days has some degree of correlation with employee health, so this data item is a possible indicator. Another possible indicator could be health-care costs (a sicker workforce utilizes more health-care services) adjusted for increases in health-care costs. Remember, indicators are associated with a particular measure, so they provide a degree of correlation when it is too difficult to measure the true variable.

It is important to be sure that the indicator being used has a strong association with the target result, or else the indicator results will prove misleading. Assume a

Noted

Indicators can be very useful ways to make a quick intervention status check when a full-blown evaluation would be too costly and time consuming at an interim stage. Check indicators biweekly to be sure everything is proceeding well, and then do a more involved evaluation at three or six months after the implementation of the performance initiative.

performance consultant seeks to evaluate management competence and uses retention as an indicator (with the belief that the better the manager, the lower the staff turnover). This indicator will not be valid in poor economic times when retention improves because there are fewer jobs in other companies to jump to, forcing employees to stay put. The original indicator (retention) would make it appear as if management competence has increased when jobs have just become scarcer.

Basic Rule 48

When forced to choose between an existing but imprecise organizational measure versus a new, more accurate metric that the business doesn't currently use, go with the existing measure. The existing metric will be credible with the client, and, because it's already being used, data collection will be easier and less expensive.

Calculating ROI

ROI has become increasingly more important to trainers (Phillips, 1991). Organizations have used ROI in the past to evaluate a number of business decisions, such as the decision whether to purchase new equipment or retool, or whether it is better to rent or own space. Other elements of the business have been expected to show ROI, so why not HRD? Consequently, there is now more pressure to show ROI on a range of different HRD initiatives. Performance consultants are positioned to use ROI to maximum effectiveness for the organization because they are capable of designing and implementing projects that show enormously high ROI rates. Also, performance consultants should choose projects based on critical business goals because their work will be more likely to yield a high ROI.

As shown in table 8-1, ROI analysis is a very useful evaluation approach in a range of situations (Phillips, 1991). In cases where an intervention is likely to be expensive because it will be implemented to a sizable workforce or because of the resource costs, ROI makes a great deal of sense. ROI is also an appropriate tool when dealing with controversial solutions or options that face significant opposition from some decision makers, and it is also a useful tool for differentiating among options.

The formula for ROI is to subtract total costs from total benefits, divide the remainder by the total costs, and multiply by 100; the result is the ROI of the project. The ROI number will be expressed as a percentage. This formula is standard

Table 8-1. When to use ROI.

If the initiative is controversial . . .	Conduct an ROI analysis!
If the initiative uses a lot of resources . . .	Conduct an ROI analysis!
If the initiative is required by law . . .	Skip an ROI analysis!
If the budget is under scrutiny . . .	Conduct an ROI analysis for key programs!
If there is a need to decide which option is best among several initiatives . . .	Conduct an ROI analysis prior to selection of the final initiative!
If the initiative enjoys wide support and is limited in scope . . .	Skip an ROI analysis!
If the initiative is a one-time effort that will not be repeated . . .	Skip an ROI analysis!
If the initiative is still being refined and improved . . .	Don't do an ROI analysis until the formative evaluation is finished!
If the initiative is similar to another that has had an ROI analysis done . . .	Skip an ROI analysis unless there is a need to compare the two initiatives!

for calculating all ROI efforts (including corporate acquisitions, IT investments, and stock returns).

Calculating the ROI really isn't that hard. First, be clear on the elements within the calculation. An ROI calculation requires information on direct costs, indirect costs, direct benefits, and indirect benefits. Direct costs involve things like prorated salaries of participants (to account for the time away from the job while participating in the intervention), cost of design (such as paying an instructional designer or graphic artist), materials (to produce the job aid or workbook), and travel costs. Indirect costs involve items that already exist but still contribute to the solution. For instance, if the organization has a training room that is used for five days in the intervention, it is an indirect cost (the intervention is paying for five days of expenses for the training room).

Direct benefits are tangible results from the intervention, such as increased sales, decreased waste, and reduced turnover rates. Indirect benefits involve intangible payoffs. As a result of the intervention, teams may become more cohesive (generally a

Basic Rule 49

It's essential to be consistent with ROI calculations and what is assigned as benefits and costs. The quickest way to destroy any credibility is to use one set of costs for some interventions and a different set for other solutions.

benefit) and people may become happier. Opportunities may also emerge if the client, for example, is now able to compete in markets that were previously closed.

As daunting as numbers can be, after you undertake ROI the first time the process becomes much easier. Internal consultants will discover that much of this data (cost per day of the training room, prorated salary of trainers) is constant and can be transferred from project to project. Also, projects that do not take participant's time in order to implement can yield astronomically high ROIs. Thus, an intervention that uses only a job aid but solves 60 percent of the problem may have an ROI of 200 percent or even 500 percent. On the other hand, training for all employees that solves 90 percent of the problem is likely to be very expensive to implement and thus have a much lower ROI, say, around 4 or 5 percent.

Noted

Here's a simple example of an ROI calculation. By providing cell phones to the salespeople, Joe's Biometrics improves close rates by 10 percent. Costs for this intervention (acquiring cell phones, paying for the plans, providing instructions/job aids for the use of the phones) turn out to be $5,000 for the year. Benefits (in terms of improved sales because of the higher close rate) turn out to be $100,000. The ROI is:

$$\frac{\$100,000 - \$5,000}{\$5,000} \times 100 = 1,900\%$$

This is an extremely high ROI, made possible because the initiative has such low expenses and the performance issue has a direct link to a measurable business goal. More common would be to find an ROI that is 8 or 12 percent.

Evaluation Mistakes

Conducting a successful evaluation can be a breeze, but that doesn't mean that you won't encounter some pitfalls, among them:

- ▶ *Measuring something because it's measurable:* Just because it's easy to count the number of hits on a Website, the number of employees who took training, average Likert scale scores on all classes for the year, or number of courses offered in the curriculum does not mean there is value in counting any of this. In fact, for the vast majority of organizations, such data is meaningless.
- ▶ *Waiting until after the intervention to begin evaluation:* Evaluation starts at the beginning of the HPI process. The further from the beginning of the process evaluation is, the harder evaluation becomes.
- ▶ *Asking the same questions and seeking the same kind of data on all interventions:* Look at why evaluation is taking place (the reason varies with each intervention), and then adapt the evaluation strategy to that purpose. That means that for some interventions you'll conduct levels 1 through 4 evaluations, others only level 1, and some will be just levels 4 and 5.
- ▶ *Failing to build evaluation into the intervention process:* If evaluation is treated as an afterthought, then clients are more likely to ignore it or refuse to support it. Build evaluation into the proposal and intervention budget. Make the case for it at the beginning of client contact.
- ▶ *Treating evaluation as something that is done primarily by the consultant:* If evaluation is being done right, most of the data necessary for evaluation is collected by the client. Use metrics that the organization already collects, use systems that are already in place, get client buy-in and support, and use client resources. That way evaluation will take less time and a large part of it will be completed by the client.

Think About This

Some clients may see little value in evaluation because they're in a hurry. Don't call the process "evaluation" when you're dealing with the client. Instead, use phrases like "next steps" or "status check."

Making Evaluation Easier

Here are some tips to simplify the evaluation process and make it more effective:

- ▶ *Use client resources where possible.* Use measures that the organization already collects data on. Look for ways to tap into systems and data collection methods that the organization currently uses and are already in place. Let the client do the heavy lifting.
- ▶ *Simplify data-collection methods.* There are a range of practical and simple ways to conduct meaningful evaluations (Hodges, 2001), such as return-on-expectations (ROE)—a form of ROI data. Evaluation does not need to be time consuming or expensive (Burkett & Phillips, 2001).
- ▶ *Push the client during front-end analysis to define a clear business goal and specific performance accomplishments.* With those elements and confidence in the root cause analysis, evaluation is easier.
- ▶ *Use a model to guide the evaluation planning and process.* Robert Brinkerhoff's (1987) evaluation model aligns well with the HPI process and provides guidance on when to evaluate and how to check the evaluation results. Kirkpatrick's approach and many other methodologies can also provide appropriate guidance. The key point is to choose a model to base the evaluation process on.
- ▶ *Avoid the evaluation mistakes mentioned previously.* Looking out for common evaluation errors has a significant impact in producing a more effective and much simpler evaluation process with better results.

Evaluation can be very simple and straightforward. However, it requires being very results focused rather than being transactional. Being good at evaluation is a powerful asset as a performance consultant; it provides support for budgets and makes it easier to decide among competing alternatives. Ultimately, evaluation is where the performance consultant brings credibility to the consultant and justifies the solution.

 ### Getting It Done

Without good reason, evaluation is one area of HPI work that is intimidating to many new performance consultants. You've discovered by now that evaluation isn't nearly as intimidating as most trainers take it to be. If you follow the basic tips covered in this chapter, you'll find evaluation is nothing to be scared about.

Exercise 8-1 offers some opportunities to deepen your understanding about evaluation and think about how to show the bottom-line impact of your interventions.

Exercise 8-1. Develop your evaluation skills.

Here are some questions that will test your knowledge of the evaluation process:

1. Choose three different interventions you've done. What would be the purpose of evaluating those interventions? Who would want the data and why would they want it? Once you've determined those answers, look at what kind of evaluation was actually done. You'll probably discover that the same questions or evaluation occurred with each initiative even though in some cases the focus should have been on formative analysis (improving the new intervention) and in other cases the focus should have been on summative evaluation (gauging the impact on the business).

2. What are the most common evaluation errors you find in your organization or by your clients?

3. Calculate the ROI for three interventions you've done. It's fine to use some estimates about data you don't have just for practice. How much do the ROI percentages vary with each solution? Try plugging in variations to each intervention (such as using a contractor versus an internal staff member) and see how the ROI changes. If you haven't used a job aid as an intervention, create a hypothetical job aid to replace a past training course and compare the ROI values for each alternative.

(continued on page 146)

Exercise 8-1. Develop your evaluation skills (continued).

4. Identify some approaches you could use to streamline your existing evaluation processes. What could you do to speed up evaluation on the work you do?

5. You may find it difficult to establish a clear link between one of your initiatives and the impact on the business, such as an increase in sales or reduced turnover rates as a result of your training. Think of several ways you can isolate the impact of your initiative on the business results.

Doing HPI work is very much about understanding and mastering the elements of performance, but there is also an element of consulting. Good consultants—whether they are financial consultants, security consultants, IT consultants, or, yes, even performance consultants—have some common competencies in dealing with clients and managing the flexibility of this kind of work. In chapter 9 you'll look at how to improve your consulting skills.

9

Putting It All Together

■ ■

What's Inside This Chapter

Here you'll see how to:

▶ Explain performance consulting to clients
▶ Choose an initial performance consulting project
▶ Improve performance consulting skills
▶ Identify resources that are especially useful to performance consultants.

Being a Performance Consultant

Becoming an effective performance consultant is more than just acquiring the necessary skills. Even with the appropriate competencies, there are still other barriers that you have to overcome to be considered a performance consultant by your peers. Most of these barriers go beyond having the skills or knowledge to actually do performance consulting. Many of these barriers are self-produced or perceptual factors in dealing with clients.

Perhaps the biggest barrier new performance consultants face in transitioning to HPI work is themselves! Most new consultants tend to wait for official permission to practice HPI and to look for approval to move forward. Waiting for those things to happen will mean waiting for a very long time to put your HPI skills to work.

Clients generally stick to what they know and the processes they are used to using. They decide what they want and then when to have HRD professionals provide it. This means new performance consultants have to step outside of their comfort zones. This may also mean challenging the status quo with clients (fighting against the transactional approach). New performance consultants can't wait for someone to give them permission to do HPI, they need to empower themselves.

Basic Rule 50

Any new performance consultant who waits to be empowered to do performance consulting will fail. HPI requires initiative, courage, and self-belief.

Selling HPI

Human resource professionals typically do a terrible job selling and explaining HPI to management and potential clients. Nothing captures the experience of how poorly professionals usually do at this job than these comments from noted performance consultant Jim Fuller (quoted in Robinson & Robinson, 1998):

> "Many professionals in training organizations have sought to transform their group from a training focus to . . . a performance improvement focus. Seeking to achieve radical organizational transformation, they create their presentation materials and march off to the boardroom to pitch the concept . . . . They have just embarked on the fastest route to failure. Experienced sales professionals would consider it the worst possible scenario—selling a product with no brand-name recognition to a skeptical customer who is not aware of what the product is, or that they even have a use for it."

This short passage demonstrates many of the things that typically go wrong in selling HPI to clients and management. HPI is not just another product or service offering. If treated that way, clients will feel free to continue demanding training (or any other intervention) instead of trying to figure out the real cause of the performance problem. Additionally, until the people providing HPI earn credibility, it's hard for business leaders to believe them when they say that HPI is going to help managers achieve business goals. Performance consultants have to clearly show potential clients how to interface with the performance function. Absent any of those components, efforts to market performance consulting will fail, and clients for the most part won't get it.

Basic Rule 51

Don't market HPI as if it were just another service. There are some unique challenges in how to sell and explain performance to management and clients. Consequently, it's necessary to approach marketing HPI differently from the method for explaining a new intervention or introducing a new training class.

The credibility of the person selling HPI is critical. Sad to say, but most executives and line managers don't view HR professionals as being savvy about the business or credible when it comes to business results. Consequently, to approach upper management about HPI, it often makes sense to look at who does have credibility with those decision makers. Don't let ego get in the way. Go with someone who has credibility (especially around business results) with senior management. The performance consultant does not need to sell the program personally. Think about who is credible with the decision makers or who can talk credibly about numbers and results with management. That's who should be pitching HPI to senior management. Consider using the following candidates to talk to senior management about HPI:

▶ union representative
▶ client or manager of the first successful HPI project
▶ manager of the department that is most critical to business success

Think About This

The critical element of approaching management about HPI is not explaining performance consulting. It is getting management to understand the need to move from a transactional approach to a results-based approach.

- ▶ chief financial officer
- ▶ former board member or advisor to senior management.

The other approach to selling HPI is *not* selling HPI. Some consultants avoid pushing the HPI approach on clients. They listen to the problem, use an HPI approach to solve it, and go on about their way. They don't talk about performance consulting or HPI concepts unless the client raises those issues. These performance consultants believe they are being hired to solve problems, not to explain concepts or models. This approach can be especially effective if the client is willing to provide some freedom or has few preconceived notions for how the work on this particular project should proceed.

Noted

You can choose from a range of approaches for explaining HPI to clients. Each performance consultant needs to decide which approach makes the most sense given the client and circumstances. Whatever approach is chosen, be absolutely clear that this is not the same challenge as adding a new training topic or intervention to the consulting toolbox. It's critical to change client perceptions about how they expect to interact with you about possible work.

Performance consultants must be able to answer the question "what is it you do?" It's important to be concise with your reply. One approach to this is an elevator speech. An elevator speech is another name for a short (approximately 30 words) description of a role or job. The most common problem with most HPI elevator speeches is they often attempt to cover all possibilities with the result being a spiel that sounds so general and all-inclusive that no one knows what it really means. A good elevator speech gives a sense of what the performance consultant does and why it's valuable. The elevator speech will probably need to change with each listener or client to make sense in various situations.

Getting Credibility

It's great if there is someone who is credible about performance to approach management or clients. But assume that isn't the case—that there is no credible surrogate.

Think About This

One effective way of explaining performance consulting is to use the Audio Logo developed by Lynn Kearney. The way the Audio Logo works is to say "I help _____ to do _____." For instance, "I help Engineering to eliminate mistakes" or "I help Customer Service to improve retention."

How can a new performance consultant acquire the necessary credibility? The single most effective way is to actually have a track record improving performance.

Basic Rule 52

Proof of success and hard data are far more persuasive about the power of HPI than words or presentations.

How can new performance consultants get proof that HPI works? Easy. They should start doing performance consulting work before they get the title and before they try to sell the concept to management. Right after reading that statement, you probably thought, "I could never do that! I don't have approval for performance consulting, and it's not on my job description."

Think back to the beginning of this chapter and remember that the biggest barriers to doing performance consulting work are self-imposed.

How can new performance consultants get proof of success if they haven't been given permission to officially perform in that role? There are at least two ways to accomplish this. First, new performance consultants can do individual roles that make up the HPI process. For instance, do the analyst role or the evaluator role on a project. Although this will not allow for the complete HPI process to be utilized, it will allow for some experience.

Some initial experience with front-end analysis work is a quick way to build a reputation as someone who is knowledgeable about the organization. There are bound to be pervasive problems in any organization that front-end analysis can offer

Basic Rule 53

Effective performance consultants are proactive. They identify performance needs and organizational priorities. They then initiate action instead of waiting for clients to come to them.

some real insight into. Once the new consultant conducts a few evaluation projects, people will begin to perceive him or her as someone who understands numbers, finances, and business impact. In any case the new consultant will have demonstrated some professional capability and won some trust in part of the process.

The second approach is the more effective way to be proactive about credibility. New performance consultants should look for an opportunity to take on a relatively small or quick project on which to use HPI (table 9-1). It should be something quick or small because the project will be done on the side. The purpose is not to attract attention; the purpose is to get some data and results with minimum fuss. These kinds of quick projects can often be found with existing clients or within the department performance consulting is part of. The project does not need to have significant impact, nor does it have to save millions of dollars. The purpose is to gain credibility and prove that the performance consultant can deliver.

It's almost impossible to find a project that meets all the criteria listed in table 9-1 for a quick win. What is important is to look for one that meets at least four of these standards. Any combination of four of those seven criteria means the project is doable for someone operating on the side and seeking a credibility-building piece of work.

Noted

Quick wins aren't necessarily easy. In terms of organizational impact, they don't have to be big wins; a quick win is a chance for you to take the first steps as a performance consultant and win some credibility. So, the decision criteria in selecting the first project revolve primarily around these questions:

- *What will provide the most credibility?*
- *What will build the most expertise as a performance consultant?*
- *What will provide an opening to a highly regarded department or credible advocate?*

Table 9-1. Picking a quick victory.

The performance consultant's first project should be one that meets at least four of the following seven criteria:

1.	Easy measurement: It won't take long to find out results, or the organization already collects the data.
2.	Clear link to measurable business results: The performers involved aren't far removed from the business result and their impact on business is easy to measure.
3.	Only limited resources are necessary to do the work: It's not a big project and something doable on the side.
4.	Short timeframe for completion: The project won't go on and on, enabling the performance consultant to gather data and implement solutions quickly.
5.	High chance of success: A small success is better than a project that could have a big impact but fails.
6.	A strong champion or a cause of major organizational pain: A strong champion will support the project through the entire process. If the performance gap is causing real pain, people are eager to see some progress.
7.	At one point the performers didn't have a performance gap: There was a time when the problem didn't exist or wasn't as big, meaning it is not a "day one" problem.

Think About This

New performance consultants can afford to be picky with their first performance consulting project. A project that leads to a training solution probably doesn't qualify for consultants who are now primarily trainers. That's because it's critical to take on a project that changes the perceptions clients have of the consultant.

Connecting to the Client

A mistake many performance consultants make is designing processes and policies without the client's perspective in mind. It is critical for potential clients to be clear about how to engage performance consultants, like who to call and what to expect once contact is made.

During the transition to HPI, it's important to make it clear to clients how to convene the performance process. In some ways, this challenge is easy. One approach is to make the performance consultant the entry point for all requests (including the more mundane ones such as getting a facilitator for a staff meeting or basic training requests). In this case, the HPI professional is the gatekeeper and decision maker. Another approach is to use the existing process (and simply take an HPI approach to analyze the requests as they come in). This does have the challenge of client expectation management if the client is used to a transactional approach and now suddenly refusing to fulfill requests will create problems.

Noted

The entry point for clients in the HPI process needs to be clear, obvious, non-intimidating, and easy to invoke. Because HPI is new for clients, the engagement process needs to be as idiot proof as possible. It must be easier for clients to get started with HPI than it is to opt for other alternatives (such as open-enrollment training, use of an external consultant, or throwing resources at the problem).

Improving Performance Consulting Skills

It's probably safe to assume anyone who has gotten this far into the book has a strong interest in performance consulting. This book has focused on being an introduction to what performance consulting is (and isn't). The following discusses how to improve and build your performance consulting skills.

It's important for new performance consultants to self-assess where they are in terms of knowledge and competencies. New performance consultants should determine which of the four HPI roles (analyst, intervention specialist, change manager, and evaluator) they're best at or provide the best fit for future work. ASTD's comprehensive 360-degree assessment tool looks at 154 competencies and terminal outputs for performance consultants (Rothwell, 1999). The number of competencies and outputs is initially daunting, but the degree of detail is incredibly useful for someone starting out in this field. This assessment could be done individually. Additionally, it ends with suggestions for personal growth tactics as well as sample developmental contracts.

Noted

No one, not even performance consulting legends like Geary Rummler or Paul Elliott, has mastered all 154 competencies and outputs. Don't be intimidated by the number of competencies and outputs. Instead, focus on the priority areas.

Once you've had a chance to either formally or informally assess your performance consulting competencies, you'll want to look at your future. How might your role change? What expectations might management have of you? The combination of your assessment and your future needs will tell you what it is you need to focus on for your development purposes.

Plenty of resources are available to improve your knowledge of performance consulting skills. ASTD provides a wide range of books on HPI. New performance consultants may also want to check out *HPI Essentials* (Piskurich, 2002), which is another book aimed at introducing HRD professionals to HPI. There are plenty of other outstanding books on performance consulting as well.

In addition, a wide range of seminars and workshops are available to boost your expertise. ASTD offers a five-course certificate series in the area of HPI. The courses in this series are

- ▸ HPI in the Workplace (an introduction to performance consulting, key theories, and models)
- ▸ Analyzing Human Performance (the analyst role and front-end analysis)
- ▸ Evaluating Human Performance (the evaluator role and measurement)
- ▸ Intervention Selection and Management (the intervention specialist and change manager roles)
- ▸ Transitioning to Performance (shaping your new practice and applying all of the concepts you've learned).

There are also a wide range of resources online. Besides ASTD's Website (www.astd.org), which includes online communities, literature searches, and books related to performance, there is the International Society for Performance Improvement (ISPI). Don Clark offers a public site (www.nwlink.com/~donclark /hrd.html) with a wide-ranging, eclectic series of content relevant to instructional systems design, performance, and training. A number of highly regarded performance consultants have Websites with plenty of accessible materials (tools, white papers, information about HPI) that are available. Several universities are getting involved in the performance arena as well.

Just remember that with any resource in the performance field—because of the performance trend, some people seek to market what they do by merely inserting the word *performance* in their title or promotional literature. Just because *performance* is in the title doesn't mean the class or book is really about performance consulting; skim materials critically before buying.

A smart performance consultant takes advantage of resources close to home. For those who are internal practitioners, you're likely to have access to professionals in the quality or OD departments who have tools and areas of expertise that are very helpful.

Connecting with others making the same journey to performance consulting will always be helpful. Do not look for one person to provide all the answers—successful performance consultants come in many models and flavors. Do not wait for approval and organizational support, because the quickest way to fail as a performance consultant is to wait for the organization to give permission and approval. Good performance consultants have skills and experience, but, more important, they have smarts, don't shy away from action, and are willing to be accountable.

 Noted

Some people want to start performance consulting by looking for risk-free transitions. This isn't possible. Being a performance consultant means being accountable for results, and thus always carries some unavoidable degree of risk.

Identifying Your Niche

The field of HPI covers a lot of ground with a range of different roles. One of the decisions new performance consultants will need to make is where to focus and what kinds of boundaries to draw. Maybe a new performance consultant will use HPI as an analytical tool but the only intervention he'll provide is training. In this situation, the performance consultant can use HPI to determine if it's a problem to get involved with or not, or the consultant can use HPI and then only provide interventions that deal with training. Or, perhaps the new performance consultant may gravitate toward particular performance consulting roles.

It also makes sense for new performance consultants to appraise how well this role fits with the talents and roles within their organization. For instance, in some firms, performance consultant are gatekeepers. Any request for an HR solution goes to the performance consultant first who then contracts with the client, gathers information, and links with other resources (such as training, benefits, recruitment, performance management staff) to generate a solution.

Conversely, there may be an OD team that claims ownership of anything having to do with teams or a group of Six Sigma Black Belts who insist that all problems with operations fall within their responsibility. How performance consultants define the HPI function and the kinds of performance projects they take on will be determined significantly by organizational dynamics, the kinds of problems the organization is facing, and internal politics. Therefore, as an internal practitioner, it's not wise to define the performance consulting function in isolation.

Instead, it will be shaped by a combination of what the performance consultant would ideally like to do, the needs of the organization, and the constraints from other forces. This shouldn't be perceived as a negative factor (or an argument against successful HPI work as an internal practitioner) because there are plenty of performance issues to go around in any organization.

Basic Rule 54

Each internal performance consulting setup is unique to that organization. Adapt the HPI function to meet the performance challenges of the firm, accommodate your organization's culture, and reflect the realities of the organizational politics.

Inevitably, however new performance consultants define their respective performance niches, it will change over time with the work they do. These changes may occur because of a real flair for certain kinds of HPI work and a decision to then focus in on those areas. Or it may be led by client demands. In addition, partnering opportunities may lead to unexpected growth. But new performance consultants should definitely expect the transition into HPI to be full of challenge, growth, surprises, and some unexpected turns.

Think About This

I'd like to say that my journey into HPI work was a result of a series of deliberate and well-informed decisions that I made sagely. In reality, I backed into doing performance work when I realized that my training just didn't change performers much. My work in this field has continued to evolve. As a performance consultant, I find it helpful to examine my niche and work focus from time to time.

Getting It Done

Pulling it all together and changing client perceptions of you and your role is tricky—but that's what this chapter is all about. Try your hand at exercise 9-1 to solidify your thinking about performance consulting.

Exercise 9-1. Finding your niche.

Here are some things you can do to apply what's been covered in this chapter:

1. Identify a quick win—a project that you can try for your first performance consulting work. Remember, you want it to meet at least four of the seven criteria mentioned in table 9-1. Ideally, you should identify several candidates. Once you've found some good potential quick wins, think through the engagement process. How will you pitch this to the soon-to-be client? What other resources would you need and who would this mean partnering with?

2. Which HPI role are you best suited for? Which HPI role is most interesting to you for future work? What skills or competencies would you need to add for that role?

3. What resources do you currently have available to improve your HPI skill set? What improvement efforts will your organization support? If you were to craft an individual development plan for yourself as a performance consultant, what would it look like?

4. What areas or performance issues do you think make the most sense for you to take on as your turf? Who might perceive HPI as a potential threat or conflict with his or her own role? What might your performance consulting niche look like?

5. What would your performance consulting Audio Logo sound like? Develop your version now. Remember, the template is: "I help _____ to do _____."

6. What would a transition roadmap look like for you if you were entering the field of performance consulting? What stages or major milestones do you see? What is the timeframe?

Congratulations! By now you should have a pretty good sense of what HPI is all about and what it takes to be an effective performance consultant. To help you along your performance journey, continue to the Additional Resources section of this book. It lists some useful publications and Websites to help you develop deeper knowledge about the performance consulting field. Good luck to you as you make the transition from trainer to performance consultant!

References

Argyris, C. (1986). "Skilled Incompetence." *Harvard Business Review, 64*(5), 74–79.

Argyris, C. (1993). *Knowledge for Action: A Guide to Overcoming Barriers to Organizational Change.* San Francisco: Jossey-Bass.

Block, P. (1981). *Flawless Consulting: A Guide to Getting Your Expertise Used.* Austin, TX: Pfeiffer & Company.

Brinkerhoff, R. (1987). *Achieving Results From Training.* San Francisco: Jossey-Bass.

Burkett, H., and P.P. Phillips. (2001). "Managing Evaluation Shortcuts." *Infoline,* No. 250111. Alexandria, VA: ASTD.

Csoka, L. (1994). "Closing the Human Performance Gap." *U.S. Conference Board Research Report,* no. 1065-94-RR.

Dean, P., M. Dean, and R. Rebalsky. (1996). "Employee Perceptions of Workplace Factors That Will Most Improve Their Performance." *Performance Improvement Quarterly, 9*(2), 75–89.

Fuller, J., and J. Farrington. (1999). *From Training to Performance Improvement: Navigating the Transition.* San Francisco: Jossey-Bass/Pfeiffer.

Gilbert, T.F. (1996). *Human Competence: Engineering Worthy Performance,* tribute edition. Washington, D.C.: International Society for Performance Improvement.

Harless, J. (1996). "Great Ideas Revisited." *T+D, 50*(1), 52–53.

Hodges, T. (2001). *Linking Learning and Performance.* Boston: Butterworth-Heinemann.

Ishikawa, K. (1969). Guide to Quality Control. Tokyo, Japan: Asian Productivity Organization.

Kepner, B., and C. Tregoe. (1965). *The Rational Manager.* New York: McGraw-Hill.

Kirkpatrick, D.L. (1975). *Evaluating Training.* Alexandria, VA: ASTD.

Mager, R.F. (1984). *Preparing Instructional Objectives.* Belmont, CA: Lake Publishing.

Mager, R.F., and P. Pipe. (1997). *Analyzing Performance Problems or You Really Oughta Wanna,* third edition. Atlanta: Center for Effective Performance.

Ohno, T. (1995). *Toyota Production System.* University Park, IL: Productivity Press.

Phillips, J. (1991). *Handbook of Training Evaluation and Measurement Methods.* Houston: Gulf Publishing.

Piskurich, G. (2002). *HPI Essentials.* Alexandria, VA: ASTD.

Robinson, D., and J. Robinson. (1996). *Performance Consulting: Moving Beyond Training.* San Francisco: Berrett-Koehler.

Robinson, D., and J. Robinson (editors). (1998). *Moving From Training to Performance: A Practical Guide.* Alexandria, VA: ASTD.

Rossett, A. (1998). *First Things Fast.* San Francisco: Jossey-Bass/Pfeiffer.

Rothwell, W. (1999). *ASTD Models for Human Performance Improvement: Roles, Competencies, and Outputs.* Alexandria, VA: ASTD.

Rummler, G., and A. Brache. (1990). *Improving Performance: How to Manage the White Space on the Organizational Chart.* San Francisco: Jossey-Bass.

Sanders, E., and J. Ruggles. (2000). "HPI Soup." *T+D, 54*(6), 26–37.

Sanders, E., and S. Thiagarajan. (2002). *Performance Intervention Maps.* Alexandria, VA: ASTD.

Willmore, J. (2002). "How to Give 'em Performance When They Insist on Training." *T+D, 56*(5), 54–59.

Additional Resources

■■

Books and Articles

Bellman, G. (1990). *The Consultant's Calling: Bringing Who You Are to What You Do.* San Francisco: Jossey-Bass.

Brethower, D. (1997). "Rapid Analysis: Matching Solutions to Changing Situations." *Performance Improvement, 36*(10), 16–21.

Brinkerhoff, R. (2003). *The Success Case Method: Find Out Quickly What's Working and What's Not.* San Francisco: Berrett-Koehler.

Broad, M., and J. Newstrom. (1992). *Transfer of Training.* Reading, PA: Addison-Wesley.

Callahan, M. (1999). "From Training to Performance Consulting." *Infoline,* No. 259702.

Callahan, M. (1998). "The Role of the Performance Evaluator." *Infoline,* No. 259803.

Clark, R. (1998). "Motivating Performance: Part 1—Diagnosing and Solving Motivation Problems." *Performance Improvement, 37*(8), 39–47.

Dent, J., and P. Anderson. (1998). "Fundamentals of HPI." *Infoline,* No. 259811.

Elliott, P. (1996). "Power-Charging People's Performance." *T+D, 50*(12), 46–49.

Fuller, J. (1997). *Managing Performance Improvement Projects.* San Francisco: Jossey-Bass.

Fuller, J. (1999). "Understanding Human Performance Improvement." In: B. Sugrue and J. Fuller (editors). *Performance Interventions: Selecting, Implementing, and Evaluating the Results.* Alexandria, VA: ASTD.

Hale, J. (1998). *The Performance Consultant's Fieldbook: Tools and Techniques for Improving Organizations and People.* San Francisco: Jossey-Bass/Pfeiffer.

Harless, J. (1989). "Wasted Behavior: A Confession." *Training, 26*(5), 35–38.

Harless, J., and P. Elliot. (1991). "Improving Performance, Achieving Goals." *Technical & Skills Training, 2*(4), 8–12.

Jackson, S. (1998). "Task Analysis." In: P. Dean and D. Ripley (editors). *Performance Improvement Interventions: Culture and Systems Change.* Washington, D.C.: International Society for Performance Improvement.

Kirkpatrick, D.L. (1994). *Evaluating Training Programs: The Four Levels.* San Francisco: Berrett-Koehler Publishers.

Koehle, D. (1999). "The Role of the Performance Change Manager. *Infoline,* No. 259715.

LaBonte, T. (2001). *Building a New Performance Vision.* Alexandria, VA: ASTD.

Langdon, D. (2000). *Aligning Performance: Improving People, Systems and Organizations.* San Francisco: Jossey-Bass/Pfeiffer.

Reinhart, C. (2000). "How to Leap Over Barriers to Performance." *Training & Development, 54*(1), 20–24.

Robinson, D., J. Robinson, and K. Blanchard. (2002). *Zap the Gaps.* New York: HarperCollins.

Rothwell, W. (2000). *The Analyst.* Alexandria, VA: ASTD.

Sugrue, B., and J. Fuller (editors). (1999). *Performance Interventions: Selecting, Implementing, and Evaluating the Results.* Alexandria, VA: ASTD.

Swanson, R. (1994). *Analysis for Improving Performance: Tools for Diagnosing Organizations and Documenting Workplace Expertise.* San Francisco: Berrett-Koehler.

Willmore, J. (2003). "Process and Results: Human Performance Improvement Identifies Causes and Solutions." *Association Management, 55*(6), 49–53.

Willmore, J. (2003). "The Seven (Actually Nine) Deadly Sins of New Performance Consultants." *T+D, 57*(8), 28–33.

Web-Based Resources

www.astd.org. ASTD's Website with a performance and evaluation online community, literature searches, books, and articles, plus information on the ASTD HPI program.

http://www.nwlink.com/~donclark/hrd.html. Don Clark's Website of free training, instructional design, and performance resources—an incredible resource.

http://edweb.sdsu.edu/edweb_folder/pt/pt.html. San Diego State University's (home of Allison Rossett) HPT Website with a glossary of terms and other useful tibits.

www.ispi.org. The Website for the International Society for Performance Improvement. Some free white papers, a superb free newsletter (*Performance Xpress*), and other useful information on performance.

www.partners-in-change.com. The Website for Dana and Jim Robinson with a mixture of useful things—some articles, tools, and models that are free and other items for a fee.